P9-DEE-042

The Man
Who Forgot
How to Read

Also by Howard Engel

FICTION

Memory Book

The Cooperman Variations

My Brother's Keeper (with Eric Wright)

Mr. Doyle and Mr. Bell

Getting Away with Murder

There Was an Old Woman

Murder in Montparnasse

Dead and Buried

A Victim Must Be Found

A City Called July

Murder Sees the Light

Murder on Location

The Ransom Game

The Suicide Murders

NONFICTION

Crimes of Passion: An Unblinking Look at Murderous Love

A Child's Christmas in Scarborough

Lord High Executioner: An Unashamed Look at Hangmen, Headsmen, and Their Kind

The Man Who Forgot How to Read

Howard Engel

Thomas Dunne Books
St. Martin's Press
New York

THOMAS DUNNE BOOKS.
An imprint of St. Martin's Press.

THE MAN WHO FORGOT HOW TO READ. Copyright © 2007 by Howard Engel.
Afterword © 2007 by Oliver Sacks. All rights reserved. Printed in the United
States of America. For information, address St. Martin's Press, 175 Fifth
Avenue, New York, N.Y. 10010.

ISBN-13: 978-0-312-38209-4
ISBN-10: 0-312-38209-X

First published in Canada by HarperCollins Publishers Ltd

In memory of Arthur A. Hamilton and Sheldon P. Zitner

The Rev. A. A. Hamilton always encouraged me in my work and I had often sharpened my wits on his original, enquiring and omnivorous mind. My friend Sheldon, known in print as the poet S. P. Zitner, stimulated me over long lunches with his crystalline, dark wit.

"Much of my unassisted self . . . I struggled through the alphabet as if it had been a bramble-bush; getting considerably worried and scratched by every letter. After that, I fell among those thieves, the nine figures, who seemed every evening to do something new to disguise themselves and baffle recognition."

—Charles Dickens, *Great Expectations*

*The Man
Who Forgot
How to Read*

MY NAME IS HOWARD ENGEL. I write detective stories. That's what I tell people when they ask me what I do. I could say I'm a writer or a novelist, but that raises a false echo in my brain, so I'm happier with the more modest claim of writing detective stories. I've written quite a few of them.

Before I started writing I was a reader. I read widely, everything from the *John, Mary and Peter* primer of my early childhood to Corn Flakes boxes when there was nothing more inspiring handy. I've been a reading junkie since public school. I played little baseball because I was searching with Lancelot for the Holy Grail and helping to free the widow's sons from the Sheriff of Nottingham's henchmen.

I came home from summer camp without a tan because of books and comic books. I was reading about astronomy before I knew where the nearest drug store was located. My universe began at *Betelgeuse*, not at Binder's Drug Store. When I came home from university, my family didn't know how to talk to me; I was so full of books, I was no longer able to understand a request to pass the salt without a philosophical discussion on the nature of joint ownership of property or state capitalism. When I lived in Europe, and I became frustrated with my lack of fluency in French, Greek or Italian, I sought out the local English bookstore.

I was in fact a very busy fellow, writing about my home town, St. Catharines, Ontario, and turning it into the murder capital of the world. Benny Cooperman, my personal private investigator, has been successful in more than a dozen novels, several short stories, radio broadcasts and two films. His name has turned up in crossword puzzles in the *Los Angeles Times*. He is doing well. Or, at least, he *was* doing well when I, the author of his being, was stricken with a sudden stroke in 2001, which put us out of the writing business by robbing me of the thing I loved above all things: the ability to read.

This book is about the road back. About how I coped, the people who helped me along the way and how I found my road back into the mysteries of what reading and writing are all about. It's a success story, in a way, because at the end of this story I am writing again. Not only that, but I have had another Benny Cooperman book published. It is a story with palpable commercial possibilities, but that is not the reason I wrote it. For me it is much more important to look back and remember all the steps that got me where I am. I need to know that so I won't forget that there was a struggle along the way and that there was a small army of people who helped me climb all those steps.

1

DAVID COPPERFIELD BEGAN HIS AUTOBIOGRAPHY with a chapter called "I Am Born." In *this* book, which is more of a memoir than an autobiography, I will not dredge up all the facts about my life the way young Copperfield did. Copperfield had a lot more trouble than I've had and he had an amanuensis, Charles Dickens, to do his heavy lifting for him. This memoir will concentrate on a significant but short period of my life. Yet in order for you to begin that part of the story, it is necessary to know who it is that is preparing to lift some of his veils and masks.

The facts of my life are simply told: I was born in Toronto, Ontario, Canada, on the second of April, 1931, in the Private Patients' Pavilion of Toronto General Hospital.

My mother enjoyed telling people that. I gather that in 1931 in Toronto the Private Patients' Pavilion was the place to be born. Lolly Greisman Engel, my mother, always liked to go first class. She almost always got it, too, whether she asked for it or not. According to family tradition and an album full of photographs, mostly falling from their triangular black moorings, I was a bright, active child with endless curiosity. One of the pictures shows me standing in underpants—which would make me one and a half years old, or two—staring up the nozzle of a garden hose in our back yard.

At my birth it was found that I had an unfinished left hand. It looked more like a paw with tiny ball-like fingers. My boyhood friend Garth Dittrich used to call it "My little doggie." My parents hauled me off to see the leading specialist in such things.

I think it may have been Dr. Alan Brown, the developer of Pablum, who also urged them to have another child as soon as possible in order to belay any growing sense of specialness or singularity in me. Enter brother David twenty-one months later. During my early days, my hand never bothered me. In fact, in spite of David's presence and Dr. Brown, I did think I was special. The hand didn't keep me from any of the activities a child gets into. And I developed a normal jealousy towards the baby of the family. I still wear the scar on my thigh from trying to climb into the high chair that had been lately mine and was now David's. I tumbled out and gouged a chunk of flesh from my leg. Despite this incident, I climbed and romped with my friends, up and down trees and across rooftops with the rest of the neighbourhood children. It was only when I became a teenager and interested in acting that my hand became a problem.

My mother, Lolly, was one of seven sisters, the family of a sewing-machine operator in the garment district of Toronto's colourful Spadina Avenue, a Canadian version of New York's Third Avenue. My father, Jack Engel, had six assorted brothers and sisters. His younger brother, Bill, was a well-known sprinter. An Olympic hopeful, he once beat the amazing American Ralph Metcalfe. While Uncle Bill was very fast on the public track, at family picnics he was usually beaten by his sister, my aunt Hannah. My father's high-school education had abruptly ended when he punched his football coach on the jaw. Unfortunately, the coach was also the school principal. He ended his teenage years selling women's hats throughout eastern Canada. Instead of becoming bitter, he developed an admiration for education in others.

Shortly before my birth, my father opened a ladies' ready-to-wear store in St. Catharines, across Lake Ontario from his Oshawa birthplace. It was 1930 and the Great Depression was upon them. The store already had a name and a big sign out front—Edward's Women's Wear—at

200 St. Paul Street, at the top of James and above the Old Canal that ran along the back of the city's main street. It was one of the best locations in town. Edward's kept the family in comfortable circumstances, sent us to summer camps, gave us holidays and put me and David through university.

My interest in the theatre began while I was still in public school, where the senior students and choir entertained the rest of us at assemblies. Edith Cavell Public School had been built across the Old Canal from the main business and residential section of the city. The school was on a tract of wasteland at the top of a gully that drained into a ravine that led to Twelve Mile Creek. The CNR station was located there, and the new (in 1930) High Level Bridge led traffic to it. On the city map our enclave was called West St. Catharines, but we knew it as Western Hill.

There is a tarnished silver cup before me as I write that has my name on it, dated 1949, one of my high-school years. It reads: "Dramatics Trophy." My uncle Bill, the runner, always used to greet me with the remark, "So, you're in plays!" And I was. In spite of the malformed left hand, I trod whatever boards that had plays on them. I played Shylock in my last year. I was an undistinguished Malvolio at McMaster University in Hamilton, Ontario, a year later. I played a dozen other characters before I decided I was not the next Laurence Olivier. But I still followed what was happening in the world of theatre.

Long before I discovered the stage, I was putting on marionette shows with my brother. Together, with the help of
friends, we put on shows in church basements, public librar-
ies and school auditoriums all over St. Catharines. We did
one show at the YMCA, where we were shocked to see all of
our schooteachers out front watching. Our most ambitious
production was a drama, in several scenes, of the story of
Jack and the Beanstalk. For this we made Jack, his mother,
the giant and a rather unconvincing cow. Other puppets
in the troupe were a dancing girl, Al Jolson in blackface,
Pépé the Clown and Meatball, a comic piano-player.

I recall one night when we were putting on a show in a
public school on Queenston Street, David and I and whoever
was helping out on that occasion, probably Don Webster,
went to get a hamburger near the canal. It was a dark, blus-
tery night in late October and we took a shortcut through
Victoria Lawn Cemetery on our way back. We frightened
ourselves telling ghost stories for half of the journey, then
ran the rest of the way with self-conjured spooky images. I
seem to remember nearly tripping over pieces of wood that
barely covered an open grave. We added a ghost to our cast
of puppet characters soon after this.

When I wasn't actually putting on shows, I read books
from the public library, beginning with those about pup-
petry. Clem Bartlett and I put together a stage that eventually stood six feet high and measured ten feet across the

curtained front. My brother, David, Wally Gillcrest and Don Webster made up the crew. I made the marionettes myself, although I had an assist from my mother in the knitting and sewing departments. Once the heads of the mari- onettes were either carved or modelled from an asbestos- like compound, hands and feet had to be fashioned. Then the strings had to be added, and they had to be attached to a control bar. I am skipping the part about making hair—I could write a whole chapter on hair. Then the faces had to be painted. The stage and boxes of marionettes were bulky enough to fill a small truck. It took us an hour to set up the stage and hang the puppets behind the scenes.

~

I DID MY FIRST WRITING FOR THESE PUPPETS. To me, writing did not seem to be a special, somewhat elevated task; it was just another of the many jobs that had to be done once the paint was dry and the hair was pasted on the puppet heads. I had to give the marionettes *words.* And that was the beginning of writing for me. No one could ever claim that I learned how to write in an ivory tower. Still, even in the magic world of Jack and his beanstalk, there were stresses and problems. For a youngster who lived not far away from losing control when strings became tangled or when my father teased me about not being available to drive some of the equipment and the crew to the church hall or library on show night, I got on very well for the most part. But there were incidents, and it was my mother who picked me up and untangled *my* strings.

The puppet show was important to me in many ways. Whatever skill I have in practical matters goes back to those days. Building the puppet theatre in the dug-out basement of an unfinished church with the help of Clem Bartlett was one of them. More importantly, preparing the marionette productions got me into writing. The puppets needed words, scripts, written material. And I had to provide it. My version of *Jack and the Beanstalk* has not survived—probably a good thing—but it did get me started in the writing game.

While all of this was going on, I was dipping deeper and deeper into the shelves at the public library. Here I started a habit that I maintained throughout my life. I became addicted to print. I have always had two or more books on the go wherever I've been. There is a book on my bedside table now, and one in the living room. In my office, I'm swamped with shelf after shelf of them. I'm an addict of the printed word.

2

I CAN SCARCELY REMEMBER A TIME WITHOUT BOOKS. Before I could read them, they were my giant building blocks. I drew pictures on the fly-leaves of my parents' books. I was so happy that the publishers supplied blank pages at the beginnings and ends of popular novels for me to draw steam engines on. The drawings show that although I had reproduced the general look of a locomotive, I had missed out on the quantitative aspect. There was no limit to the number of wheels, bells and bumps I added to the silhouette of a train engine. I could be inventive with the alphabet as well. I taught myself to make black marks that stood for letters. When I was pretending to write a piece I knew by heart, I tried to get my recitation to end at the same time as I wrote the last words. It was Miss Alton at Edith Cavell Public School who properly taught me to read and to write.

My first book was a collection of Mother Goose nursery rhymes, which sits beside me as I write this. It is spineless and incomplete, with tattered binding and torn pages. But somehow it has managed to stay with me down through the years. The strong illustrations stand out now as they did when I first opened the book when I was three or four. I asked Margaret Maloney, who was once in charge of the Osborne Collection of Early Children's Books at the Toronto Public Library what she could tell me about the book. I thought that the knobbly English faces would immediately announce the name of a well-known illustrator from the 1880s. But no. There wasn't much she could tell me. It wasn't a rare book, except to me, and I will continue to treasure it.

I still find inspiration in it because these were the first pages I learned to read by myself. Take, for example, the form of "The House That Jack Built." It's a kind of cumulative narrative that goes back to an ancient Hebrew form, still sung around the Passover table in Jewish homes, and in naughty verses about male prowess beginning "We were fifteen days out of Port Darwin . . ." Another of the nursery rhymes was about the old woman and her pig who couldn't get home until a score of things happened first. She complained:

Ox, ox, drink water:

Water won't quench fire,

Fire won't burn stick,

Stick won't beat dog,

Dog won't bite pig,

Piggy won't get over the style.

And I shan't get home tonight.

The old woman ends this long train of intractability when she fills a leaky bucket with pebbles so that it will hold water enough to refresh the cow. Then: "the cat began to kill the rat, the rat began to gnaw the rope, the rope began to hang the butcher . . ."

My father always fell asleep under the spread-out print of the *Toronto Daily Star*. My younger brother and I had to dig our way through print to get him to tell us the story about his fictional adventures in *darkest Africa*. My mother read novels all the time and shared some of them with me at an early age. Her favourites were historical novels, like *Forever Amber, Leave Her to Heaven* and *The Sun Is My Undoing*. I suppose that many of them would now be called "bodice rippers." She also read Proust, because, she told me, she liked family stories.

When my father acquired the contents of a lending library, our reading branched out. There was a biography of the French spy from the First World War, Mata Hari. I was very moved by her brave end. Somehow my father found and brought home most of an encyclopedia in about twenty volumes. When I discover that there are areas of knowledge of which I know nothing, I often blame the missing volumes. The books contained a few modern photographs, of politicians from around the time of World War I, but most of the illustrations were steel engravings of stern, unsmiling male faces, growling at the world. The books must have come from the States, because they made a great fuss about the American presidents. I still remember that the article on Washington said, "Providence left him childless so that a nation might call him father."

Later came the Grolier Society's *Books of Knowledge*, with its fenced-globe colophon. David and I had favourite volumes: he liked the one with a large black Newfoundland dog in it, and I preferred the articles on things to make and things to do. I remember reading here Christina Rossetti's "Goblin Market" and a long story by Ruskin called "King of the Golden River," which meandered through several volumes of the set of blue-covered books. I liked the historical pictures, too: young Walter Raleigh talking to a sailor pointing out to sea, youthful Peter the Great working on the English docks. There were a few sepia plates of birds and flowers, but most of the illustrations were in a murky black-and-white, which gave the impression that all of European history happened after dark, which probably isn't far from the truth.

While I learned to struggle through *Barney Blue-Eyes* on my own, my mother encouraged my reading by filling me full of *Tom Sawyer* and, later, *Huckleberry Finn*. I was also exposed to regular doses of Arthur Ransome, Beatrix Potter and Kenneth Grahame. After a time we read all of the Howard Pyle books about King Arthur and the Round Table. I was astonished, years later, to learn that my earliest reading coincided exactly with that of the writer Mary McCarthy. As she once told a group at Harbourfront's reading series, this early reading shaped her interest in writing. It hit me the same way, not so many years later.

When I was little, I loved being read to, of course, like most children. I still like it. I had my share of Mother Goose, who led me through the Brothers Grimm and Hans Christian Andersen. Hearing the words of *The Secret Garden* or *The Prince and the Pauper* and sharing them with another was heaven. Robert Louis Stevenson's *Kidnapped* and *Treasure Island* kept me out of the sun for weeks, as did *The Story of a Bad Boy*. Not only did I swallow the texts of these books but I loved the illustrations that went with them. Later on there was a parade of Mark Twain books. Some my mother read to me, but I recall getting through most of *Huckleberry Finn* by myself.

Through my art teacher, Prynce Nesbitt, the portrait painter, I began reading more widely. A discussion about evolution led to my reading *Origin of Species* and *The Descent of Man*, long before I could properly understand them. Nesbitt led me to *Lives of the Poets* and lots of other books. I was with him one day when he met the local author Louis Blake Duff, who said to Prynce, "I believe that we are the only people within a hundred miles who have ever heard of *The Yellow Book*." Needless to say, I looked it up at the library the same day.

My mother was a constant reader, but she was never a narrow one. Kathleen Windsor, Ben Ames Williams and Frank Yerby were for everyday reading, books to enjoy with her *mah-jong* friends. She enjoyed reading me Van Loon's *Lives*, an easy entry into biography. She introduced me to Ellery Queen, Rex Stout, Dashiell Hammett and Raymond Chandler, and I have been a devoted mystery reader ever since. I didn't catch up with Arthur Conan Doyle until I heard Basil Rathbone and Nigel Bruce go at the Holmes canon on the radio a few years later.

3

AT McMASTER UNIVERSITY I MADE MY HOME at the Board of Publications, an old army H-hut, part of which produced *The Silhouette*, the weekly campus newspaper. Here I made lifelong friends. My mother calls us "the class that refused to graduate" because we continued to be friends long after we left the university.

My essays were often late because I got lost reading about some adjacent subject in the stacks at the library. When I moved my chair to a place where I might not be distracted, like the engineering section, I found myself intrigued by the story of the Quebec Bridge disaster. I lived to feel the wrath of the university librarian because I had so many books on loan while I attempted to complete the research for a paper of some sort. I read widely, omnivorously at McMaster. Everybody was always suggesting authors: "Have you tried reading Antonin Artaud?" "Do you know Tennessee Williams?" "What about John Wyndham?" "How much Joyce Cary have you read?" "Surely you've read Rabelais?" It was hard to keep up. One would be invited to sip Lapsang Souchong tea in the sitting room of a professor and to express opinions based upon wide reading. Reading was the only way to survive in such circumstances. If reading hadn't been a well-established part of my life by that time, I could never have survived.

After graduation—a near run thing—I went to teach high school for a year in Sault Ste. Marie, Ontario, before beginning a term freelancing at the Canadian Broadcasting Corporation in Toronto. I got into this after selling rush-seat tickets to *My Fair Lady* on the streets of New York. Scalping, they call it, but each scalped ticket allowed me another handful of days in Manhattan seeing plays and visiting galleries and museums. It was worth sleeping on the street in front of the box office every few nights. And when I got back to Toronto, after a month on 54th Street, I had a story to tell. I told it well enough that a reputable representative of the CBC asked me to go out to find other stories for the new program *Assignment,* with Bill McNeil and Maria Barrett. I'd met the show's executive producer, the legendary Harry J. Boyle, in the Everene Hotel pub. Boyle was the Orson Welles of Canadian broadcasting. After we talked, he offered me a job that opened out and evolved into twenty years in broadcasting. I became one of a group of freelancers known at the corporation as "Boyle's Irregulars." Because Harry drank and the brass were always on the lookout to get rid of him, he had to produce one brilliant idea after another to stay on the payroll. He started some of the best-remembered programs: *CBC Stage, Wednesday Night, Assignment,* and many more shows that not only engaged an audience but stretched the potential of radio across Canada.

I ran around with a tape recorder and pushed my microphone into the faces of movie stars and politicians. Once I got the recorded interview back to the studio, I had to edit the tape and prepare a script that would introduce the interview and then give the announcer something to say afterwards. The material could come from part of the interview that was not recorded or perhaps from something that had been cut from the item because of length. At all events, the material had to be turned into a script. It might be only "Here is Archbishop Makarios in Nicosia, Cyprus, talking about his plans for the newly independent former British colony . . ." After the tape came the "back announce" as we used to call it: "You have just heard President Makarios of Cyprus telling your correspondent about . . ." However short or long these bits of script, they had to be *written*. It was training for a writing career, even though I was unaware of it at the time.

Another blessing that came from my early experience of such radio programs as *Assignment*, Bob Weaver's *Anthology* or *The Arts in Review* or Bernie Lucht's *Ideas* was the realization that broadcasting takes place in *time*. A writer in radio learns to compose with economy: it's impossible to squeeze a thirty-second speech into fifteen seconds without distorting it. A broadcaster learns to edit, to economize, to keep to the subject. He learns discipline while developing his craft.

Somewhere in those noisy CBC offices, with laughter, shouting and carrying on, I learned to type and was encouraged to try other programs. In the insidious way that corporations turn their creative people into minor bureaucrats, I was eventually shifted to becoming an "executive producer," which meant I had to filter my creative ideas through others.

~

IT WAS FUNNY: Harry Boyle was paying me for what I might have done anyway. In time, I went from getting ideas for programs to writing them. The busy office of *Assignment*, with its broadcasting booth and control room, its reporters coming and going, was as far as one can get from the proverbial ivory tower where writers are supposedly born and nourished.

I went from researching to writing, and from writing to producing programs in radio. I had grown up listening to the CBC programs, the dramas, the readings of short stories and the wonderful documentaries that made Canadian radio renowned the world over. The most lively artifact of that period is a hard-to-find recording of a spoof on the reign of the junior senator from Wisconsin, Joseph McCarthy, called "The Investigator," in which the politician tries ridding Heaven of its left-wing element.

Almost all of my early writing was for a practical purpose: I supplied the "Here is" and "That was" portions of script that sandwiched an interview. Apart from a few attempts at writing short stories, I wrote no fiction. This was odd, seeing that in time I had become the producer of the flagship literary program on the network, *Anthology*, created by Robert Weaver. In this job, putting together new works, mostly by Canadians, with interviews with poets and writers of short stories, non-fiction and novels, with a few other things thrown in, I was beginning to feel like a eunuch in a harem: I saw the trick done every day, but I wasn't doing it myself.

I saw writers come and go from our studios, I met and became acquainted with some of the best writers in the English language, a number of whom became lifelong friends. My two wives became writers. Wherever I've lived, on whatever continent, all horizontal space has supported a pile of books.

∼

ALTHOUGH I WAS ENJOYING MY WORK under Harry Boyle, I had promised myself years earlier that I would go to Europe. That's how I came to be a foreign correspondent, working in London, Paris, Cyprus, West Germany and Spain. During my time freelancing overseas for the CBC—that would be in London, 1962—I married an old McMaster friend, Marian Passmore, who later published novels and stories under the name Marian Engel. We became parents of twins, William and Charlotte. When the marriage ended sixteen years later, I began writing myself. It was while I was married to Janet Hamilton, my second wife, that things began to happen with my writing.

One evening, after a good dinner, I left Janet to entertain our guest, a dear friend, Chaviva Hosek, while I went to my office to putter. I say I went to putter because puttering is the only thing that had come out of that room in several years: the odd poem or magazine article or review, certainly not a body of work. I sat down in front of my typewriter—of course, it was all manual in those days—just to see what I could do. Sitting there, I wanted to see how far I could go. At the end of an hour, I found I had written seven or eight pages, which were the beginnings of my detective Benny Cooperman and whatever I can boast of as a literary career.

I never found the actual writing easy. My fingers stumbled over the keys. My head was full of misgivings. "Can I finish the page? Can I add another hundred words to the total?" To my surprise, when the writing was going well, it seemed that all I had to do was remove the filled pages and insert a new blank one. When my mind froze up, writing can only be compared to trying to move a ton of raw liver uphill by hand. At the end of five weeks, I had a very rough manuscript, and it had a beginning, a middle and an end.

At first I had no plot, no characters, nothing. I didn't even know what sort of book—if it was going to be a book—would develop. I had always enjoyed reading crime fiction, even as a child, so why not start there? Sherlock Holmes, Sam Spade, Philip Marlowe and company—could I join their mighty fellowship? I was just devious enough to try.

I decided that my detective would be the opposite of all the detectives that existed at that time. Most detectives, both professional and amateur, were from large cities: London, New York, Los Angeles, San Francisco. They were at least nominally Christian. (I don't know about Charlie Chan.) They were tough, slick, heavy-drinking womanizers, every one of them, except, maybe, Ellery Queen.

Benny Cooperman, on the other hand, was Canadian, Jewish and devoted to chopped-egg sandwiches. He side-stepped alcohol, was shy and unfamiliar with fisticuffs. Benny came from a city of seventy- or eighty-thousand souls on the Canadian side of the border close to Niagara Falls. My model was my own hometown of St. Catharines, the place I knew best. I changed the name to Grantham so I could move the streets around a little, and confuse critics, but kept the place mostly like the original.

Where most fictional detectives treated the finding of dead bodies all in a day's work, Benny was sick at the sight of blood and headed for the nearest washroom. Where they were clever at solving puzzles, Benny did his serious digging at the local Carnegie Library. Benny began in my imagination as an assortment of opposites, a mechanical mixture of negative qualities, but, from the very first time he opened his mouth to speak, surprisingly, he did so in his own distinctive voice.

When I wrote that handful of pages that night when the dinner company spared me, and I brought it down for approval, I was sent back to finish what I had started. In fact, that first handful of pages became the beginning of my first novel. This might be seen as remarkable when it is known that until that moment the longest piece of writing that I had ever published was an eleven-page poem about the Welland Canal.

At first Benny is the equivalent of the newspaper on the bottom of a bird cage of the business: he does all the dirty work. He follows paper trails, he tracks spouses and reports back to the husbands and wives. They pay him to stand under dripping eavestroughs trying to record conversations behind the closed blinds of the Black Duck Motel out on Number 8 Highway. To some people, Benny is a bit of a *schlemiel,* someone not to be taken too seriously, but it is just that quality that makes him so good. Over the years, Benny has become very accomplished at what he does. No longer is he recommended by Anna Abraham's housekeeper, or the wino Kogan, the handyman in his office building. He gets better, more respectable cases.

Professionally, Benny works alone. But sometimes he lets the local librarian do his digging for him in the library stacks. And occasionally, more often than they know, his friends Staziak and Savas, both ornaments of the Niagara Regional Police, do some of the legwork that comes with Benny's current job. His friends, the cops, take Benny to local eateries to extend his knowledge of food and restaurants. (Benny left home with memories of his mother's bad cooking as his only legacy.)

Benny is a homebody who now lives in a rented room, having exhausted himself in moving away from the family. His older brother is a successful Toronto surgeon. And his parents never let him forget it. Benny does not golf or lift weights. His favourite sport is watching old movies. While his mother can't understand the point of his becoming a "freelance policeman," his girlfriend, Anna Abraham, a professor at the local university, finds something in him to admire and love. Benny, whose education stopped at the end of high school, is fascinated by Anna and the crowded parking lots surrounding Secord University. He is all for anything that inspires so much driving.

At heart, Benny is a tidier. He likes to clean up messes, to restore order. He does this in all of his stories. But, while he is tidying and straightening, Benny's own life is in shambles. His life is like his messy office. As his father might say, "He's got merchandise mixed up all over the store." With all his deficiencies, Benny is a better detective than he thinks he is. Although he often seems to be in a muddle, his methods pay off, as he might have guessed himself if he noticed the quality of the cases improving from adventure to adventure.

Benny has been a good companion over the years. Not once did I feel that he was cramping my style. Never have I thought of sending him over Reichenbach Falls in the wake of Sherlock Holmes. But comparison with Holmes was a long way off when I first drove up to the Sleuth of Baker Street bookstore on an evening in 1980 to attend my first book-launch party. I worried all the way. I hadn't seen the cover. When I arrived, all my problems vanished on seeing the window full of my book and my name written in large letters on every one of them.

This was the beginning of a fruitful time. One book followed another, almost a book a year through two decades. At first it was hard doing a full day's work in broadcasting and then going home to work after dinner until midnight on what might or might not turn into a saleable manuscript. It meant I had to cut into the time I spent with friends, going to movies and plays and thinking of foreign parts. In the mid-eighties I left the CBC, which had been so good to me, to make it on my own. There was a scary thrill in being independent after having a place to fall back on. I had been told since I was twelve that one should always have something to fall back on. Now I was walking a tightrope without a net. All in all, it was fun, being a writer, finding that I wasn't alone—that there were others like me struggling in the same direction.

~

AS I TYPE THESE WORDS, I am surrounded on three sides by towering bookshelves. The piles of unshelved books that surround my work table embarrass me daily, although I have contacted a carpenter who has promised to dig me out of this inundation of bound print. I feel like New York's legendary Collier brothers, one of whom was eventually crushed by the weight of their collections of newspapers and books. Such a fate may lie in store for me. It would be a fitting conclusion, like the poor fellow in E. M. Forster's *Howards End*.

~

WHEN JANET DIED OF A BRAIN TUMOUR IN 1998, I was supported through the dark days by Jacob, our eight-year-old son, and by my two older children. For a long time I buried myself in work, no longer being able to handle other aspects of my life very well, and took refuge from despair in a relationship with a Toronto woman, whom I'll call Laura.

That brings us to the year 2001. I was a published, working writer, with editions in a dozen foreign countries. I had a house with a son on the brink of his teens, and had just finished writing a fun book with my friend Eric Wright called *My Brother's Keeper*.

Everything was coming up roses once again, when I got up one morning and found things changed utterly. I could no longer read.

4

IT WAS A HOT MIDSUMMER MORNING IN TORONTO. I was
at home. My son Jacob was asleep in his bed when I stirred
long enough to collect the morning paper from the front
porch. I found out about my difficulty by chance. The July
31, 2001, *Globe and Mail* looked the way it always did in
its make-up, pictures, assorted headlines and smaller cap-
tions. The only difference was that I could no longer read
what they said. The letters, I could tell, were the familiar
twenty-six I had grown up with. Only now, when I brought
them into focus, they looked like Cyrillic one moment and
Korean the next. Was this a Serbo-Croatian version of the
Globe, made for export? What was going on here?

At first I thought it might be a trick. Was I the victim of a practical joke? I have friends who are capable of such things. I thought of them and what I would say to them when we met. I wondered what I might do to them that would improve on this piece of foolery. Then, I considered the alternative possibility. I checked the *Globe*'s inside pages to see if they looked as strange as the front page. I checked the want ads and the comics. I couldn't read them either. What made matters worse, I couldn't see the end of the line I was trying to read. The word or words beyond the point I had reached in my slow attempts at deciphering a text simply were not there. White paper was all I could see; no print. Where I could make out the text, the letters of the words appeared as though I was trying to make them out through a heat haze; the letters wobbled and changed shape as I attempted to make them out. What looked like an *a* one moment looked like an *e* the next and a *w* after that. It was like astigmatism on a drunken weekend. Through my eyes a checkerboard became op-art.

Panic should have hit me like the proverbial ton of bricks. But instead I was suffused with a reasonable, business-as-usual calm. "Since this isn't somebody's idea of a joke, then, it follows, I have suffered a stroke." It seemed the only explanation. "If not A, then B." Without panic, I thought about my life as I'd known it: "Since there is no help, come let us kiss and part . . ."

Logic. Calm. Business not *quite* as usual. Apart from the strange, twisted look of letters on a page (I kept testing myself to see whether it might not go away, or that maybe books would behave better than the newspaper), I was shocked to see that everything else had its old familiar look: the chair looked like the chair, the bed like the bed I knew and loved. Beyond the window frame, the trees outside, the black and grey squirrels, the neighbour's cat, everything looked normal. It was an ordinary day, and my perceptions of the day were as I remembered they should be. I threw some peanuts to the squirrels, and closed the door.

Panic was still giving me a wide berth. And at the same time, a censor somewhere in my brain was simplifying things for me, helping me to cope with the necessary. For instance, Jacob, my youngest son, and I were due that day to go off to the French River cabin of a good friend. Not for a moment did I think of it. It wasn't a matter that needed serious thought at that moment. It would keep, and my brain filed it away until later. Nor did I think of my friend and companion, Laura, who was off in Turkey, visiting the historic sites. My instincts seemed to be favouring simplicity. Don't complicate matters. I was like a dying cat: I sought out a quiet place in which to get on with it without panic or excitement.

I looked at the clock; it was eight-thirty, only ten minutes after I went out on the porch to collect the newspaper.

"Good!" I thought. "I can still tell time. *It* hasn't got me there yet." My unnatural calm protected me from details, from diversion.

Jacob, then about twelve, was asleep upstairs. I woke him, suggested that he shouldn't panic, but urged him to get dressed. In a very few minutes we were hailing a cab on Bloor Street. Jacob, too, had come in under the umbrella of this unnatural calm. We hardly spoke. I told him what had happened and we both sat back in the taxi to gather strength for the next stage of the adventure.

It's not a long drive from our house to the Emergency door at the hospital. But the ride confused me. I was seeing familiar landmarks in unfamiliar places. It was as though the driver was giving us a tour of the city before finding the right door on University Avenue. It was almost a surreal feeling, snapshots of reality interrupting a dreamlike, distorted vision of my view from the back seat, as though time had speeded up and rushed me faster than the taxi to my destination. I felt like Joseph Cotton as Holly Martins in *The Third Man*, having been driven at breakneck speed through the bomb-scarred streets of Vienna to the appointed lecture hall. While the effect of this on me was not unlike the experience of drunkenness, at each separate moment I seemed to be in control and looking at an ordinary world going about its early-morning business.

At the Emergency door of Mount Sinai Hospital, the

closest hospital where I was known—if a plastic card in my wallet constitutes being known—I paid off the taxi and we headed in to begin what might have been a short wait. It may also have been a long one. By now, my sense of time was beginning to crumble. My recollection is that it wasn't long.

In the waiting room, I was hailed by a colleague of my brother, a dentist who remembered me. I took some comfort in the fact that my trouble now had company. I didn't recognize the face of my brother's friend, but that was just the beginning. I've failed to recognize a thousand faces since. The dentist, Dr. Harry Rosenberg, had suffered a stroke, too, and his wife was by his side. Jacob supplied all of us with coffee from the machine and made a few telephone calls to alert close friends and my in-laws; my own family—uncles, aunts and cousins—now seemed both remote and elderly. As we sat being interviewed by the nurse, Jacob had answers to the questions my mind wasn't working fast enough to supply. When asked, I think I was unable to pinpoint my exact relationship to Jacob, which puzzled me more than it alarmed me. During this interview, I forgot my name, my age, my address and a dozen other things that Jacob calmly supplied. I was examined and sent for a battery of tests, which confirmed my own diagnosis. It was a stroke, left side, rear.

~

FOR A TIME I THOUGHT THAT, having failed to answer all the questions posed by the nurse handling admissions, I might be excused a moment of panic. But it failed to come. Except for the fleeting of surprise when I failed to find my name, my age or my occupation, I was subject to a soothing calm that removed from me the frustration and fear that such lapses might be expected to trigger in me. It was as though my sphere of consciousness had become elastic: it settled snugly around me, giving me a sense of well-being I had no business experiencing. Maybe my sensation of ease was akin to the calming protection that takes heroes into the line of fire and parents into a burning building to save a child.

We sat in the Emergency waiting room until a bed could be found for me. When it was, we were welcomed by the staff of the Strokes and Brain Injuries floor and settled in a room. I was happy that I could see the nursing station from where I lay. And the following day I was visited by my own family doctor. What could go wrong under such circumstances?

The first days at Mount Sinai moved me through a series of tests and examinations. I was much probed and pounded, saw the insides of X-ray and MRI machines. Blood and blood pressure were taken religiously. My blood pressure seemed to give the staff more trouble than I was worth.

I never knew how moody these things could be. At first I thought that they took my blood pressure so often because they lost the notation from last time. Later I learned that it was because the blood pressure changed from moment to moment. I felt like a tropical fish that showed his changing moods through his colouration.

I began to look about me and take in my surroundings. Different people fed me and bathed me. A propped-up pillow or a bedpan were only a bell-buzz away. They even fed me from time to time. A tray was regularly brought to my bed.

It was during this early phase of my stay at Mount Sinai that I first heard the medical term for my problem. It was a collection of Greek or Latin words. Alexia something-or-other. Of course, I didn't take in their meaning. Not the first time the name was mentioned. Not the second or third either. A nurse told me that it meant that I was no longer able to recognize printed symbols—that, in fact, I could no longer read.

What was I to do with such news? I was a *writer*! That's what I *did*. I had written a dozen books. I was even moderately well known for it. I had the statuettes to prove that I'd even won awards. I felt like a plumber told to stay clear of drains and lead pipes, or a banker told to avoid dealings with money. The stroke couldn't have hit me in a more personal place above the waist.

When I'd caught my breath from that body blow, she went on to assure me that, while I couldn't read, I could still write. I began having thoughts about what to tell my publishers. "I can still write, but I can't read. I'll write you a book, but I don't do rewrites as a matter of principle." How was I going to support myself and Jacob? Was it time to start begging in the streets? Like poor Christian at the beginning of *Pilgrim's Progress*, I asked myself, "What shall I do?" I saw myself as the only illiterate in the literary community. I saw my work, which I had been toiling at since 1980, with the old journalist's symbol:

–30–

a mark written at the bottom of the final page meaning: "That's all there is. There isn't any more."

5

MY MEMORIES OF MY TIME IN MOUNT SINAI, and later the Toronto Rehabilitation Hospital, remain vague and confused. They have become mixed up, overlapping and perhaps even reinvented. Did this happen in the hospital or in rehab? Where was it that the shower was down the hall? In which place was I first allowed out of bed? Like pentimento images, they bleed one into the other and confuse me with having to sort them out. The term *pentimento* comes from paintings in which the underpainting has started showing through the artist's second thoughts. There is a description in *Huckleberry Finn* of a painting that is confused by too many arms sketched onto the canvas, which give the subject, in Huck's opinion, a rather squid-like appearance. So it is with my tangled memories of the two institutions that looked after me. I was in the first place for not much more than a week; I was in Rehab for nearly three months, with return visits to pursue further therapy.

An example might be cited to give the reader a glimpse of my confusion. In my room at Mount Sinai the bathroom contained a shower stall. Whenever I used the bathroom later at the Rehab, which didn't have a shower, I found that it was "missing." My memory was out of sync, out of sequence, like a badly stacked deck of cards. When I ran into this kind of mix-up, and I often did, I felt as though I was watching a film in which the soundtrack no longer matched the lip movements of the characters.

By now I was aware of other confusions, too: I mixed things up. For one thing, I could no longer remember the names of my visitors. No sooner did I begin searching for a name, even that of a family member or a good friend, than, like a trout, it slithered away. Sometimes it seemed that all the proper nouns in my personal directory were sitting on the tip of my tongue, my crowded tongue, and I was incapable of capturing any of them.

Sorting out the staff was another difficulty. I mixed everybody up. All women in uniform I called "nurse," and I was wrong most of the time. Nurses took my pulse and temperature, but the similarly clad women who emptied the garbage beside my bed, or gave me a cookie at bedtime, were not quite nurses. I'd heard of volunteers called candy-stripers but never saw one. Female doctors usually wore lab coats, and sometimes they came dressed to go off to a cocktail party. The male doctors were easy to spot. They never travelled the corridors alone. They moved with a phalanx of lesser beings—nurses and interns. "Left, right, left" they came, in a no-nonsense formation, like soldiers being drilled on a parade ground. They all hovered at the foot of every bed while the doctor checked the chart. To the patient he was affable, even friendly; to the entourage he spoke with a different voice.

One thing is certain: I shared the space with another human being. I had a roommate, who was occupied by his own troubles, which were far worse than mine. He never said a word to me the whole time I was with him. He just lay there in his bed, barely responding to the visitors who regularly crowded his side of the hanging curtain that separated us. I never learned his name or found out what brought him to the hospital. His visitors were encouraging in what they said to him, but I never heard more than an indecipherable, reedy response from the patient. I never even learned his name. This may speak more of my own preoccupations than of the seriousness of his condition.

I had been placed in the hospital's stroke unit. Here I learned that my stroke was called an "insult" to my brain. The doctors and nurses kept saying that the patient "presented" such and such an appearance, as though we were showing off our medals on Canada Day.

Throughout the week's stay at Mount Sinai, I never lost that serene calm. It protected me from the harsh realities I wouldn't have wanted to think about anyway: What was I going to do for a living if I couldn't read? What was going to happen to Jacob? Who was paying my bills? Did my doctor know what my poor head was doing?

While at Mount Sinai, I heard the answer to this last question. What ailed me was expressed in three foreign words, which I had trouble remembering. I couldn't hold on to the words. I tried harder; after all, the words were singularly important to me. What I had was alexia sine agraphia. It took me a while to pronounce it, and even longer to remember the name. What alexia sine agraphia means is that while I am still able to write without difficulty, I can no longer read what I have written. It is a rare condition, rare enough to catch the interest and imagination of most of the people I would be working with both at Mount Sinai and at Rehab.

Alexia is the dark twin of aphasia. Aphasia, which is a disturbance in language, was never my problem. I could always, and still can, talk a conversation to death. My problems were wholly visual. My problem with writing, which I discovered much later on, was holding a complicated structure in my head long enough to get it all down on paper. But that is leaping ahead too far and too quickly.

The alexia was the chief thorn in my side. The sine agraphia was the sop designed to make me feel good. It was like being told that the right leg had to be amputated but that I could keep the shoe and sock.

Along with the alexia, it was found that my vision had been affected by the stroke as well. I had lost a quarter of my vision in the upper right-hand side of the visual screen. Draw a circle, quarter it, and black out the top right quadrant. Three quarters of my vision was intact; the remaining quarter was not paying its way. After taking a test where I was asked to press a button whenever I saw a pinpoint of light, I was shown that I failed to notice the light when it appeared in the upper right side of the visual field. Oddly enough, I didn't notice this huge blind spot.

Human vision is very good at faking the scene. For instance, if you and I are looking at a sheet of evenly coloured cloth, the image I see is what you see, for the area that my eye doesn't register is filled in and blended with the rest by my brain. My visual defect is cleverly swept under the carpet; like a chameleon, the brain adds the missing colours, filling in the gaps. We all know the old trick that helps discover the normal blind spot on the retina—you stare at an **X** on a piece of paper and gradually move it towards you until a nearby ● vanishes where the optic nerve itself connects with the retina. And in your case, too, the brain fills in the blind spot so you "see" a complete scene. In my case, there are many such blind spots.

Nature has a way of making silk purses out of our sows' ears. We see better than we should, or at least our blind spots are hidden from us except when we go looking for them. In a more general sense, I have found, most of my difficulties work the same way. For instance, I am not aware as I go through my day that I can no longer remember the name of the author Graham Greene. It is only when I am asked directly who is the author of *The Third Man, Brighton Rock* or *Dr. Fischer of Geneva* that I become aware of my difficulty with the name. I know the name well; I once could spout dialogue from the film of *The Third Man*, but, put on the spot, I discover the name is dangling just out of reach on the tip of my tongue. If I had to face all my similar deficits, as they call them in the hospital, I would be plunged into an irreversible depression, I'm sure. But as it is I am protected by nature from looking at all my defects at once. I am aware of them only when I reach for a name or an idea and find it missing.

So, when I wasn't trying to read a paper or a get-well card, the alexia didn't bother me. The sky looked blue, the sun shone on the hospital windows, the world hadn't suddenly become unfamiliar. My alexia existed only when I had my head buried in a book. Print brought it on and reminded me that, yes, there was a problem. Thus was born the temptation to simply avoid reading. If something bothers you, stay away from it and the world will continue to turn. Such a solution might work for some, but it could never work for me. I was a writer. And I have always been a reader. How could I stop?

In the hospital, I found that, even though the reading was slow and difficult—frustrating as hell at times—I was still a reader. The blast to my brain could not make me otherwise. Reading was hard-wired into me. I could no more stop reading than I could stop my heart. Reading was bone and marrow, lymph and blood to me.

~

WHILE I WAS BEGINNING TO DEAL WITH MY ALEXIA, I had to catch up on what had been happening to my son Jacob. When he visited, he told me that he had spent the first two nights of my hospitalization with his grandparents in north Toronto. From there he went to two of his former schoolteachers, both good family friends. From there he moved to a website-designer's house, and from there to the house of a school pal. It was a peripatetic life, living out of a duffle bag and knapsack, but it was new and a bit of an adventure for him. He visited me almost every day. In fact, my hospital room had become the exchange point, the place where he switched hosts and hostesses.

These domestic arrangements worked perfectly and they functioned mostly without my participation. Jacob and his friends and relatives had formed themselves into a network that operated without any—or at least very little—input from me. Apart from not having his own things about him, he said he managed very well. He always had something to tell me when he visited. Who paid for all of this, I never did find out.

My vagueness about where my son was living at a given moment seems a serious flaw in an otherwise devoted parent. But this lack of clarity was also part of what was happening in my head. Discrete vaguenesses had crept into my mind. Time, for instance. Days, weeks, months went by more quickly than I can ever remember them. Time dwindled and evaporated. I don't recall losing great chunks of time—the forgetting of doctors' visits, or trips to other hospitals for tests—but I feel as though an editor has been working behind me, snipping the longueurs and idle times out of my life. As a consequence, I could never tell whether it was Tuesday or Thursday, whether it was March or September. Part of this, I know, has to do with being institutionalized. One day is so much like the last. But it was more than that. For, while we *were* removed from the haunts of men, the business and bustle of the city, we did keep up with what was happening in the world. My visitors kept me abreast of the news of my little world of neighbours, writers and the headlines.

My companions on the fifth floor were well read and well

travelled, so our talk was about outside events, not merely a catalogue of bypasses, transplants and impairments. We talked of our travels in the world, of diplomatic postings, and how we ended up in Canada. We were all trying to keep a grip on the real world and the parts we played in it.

But my real world was not quite like its predecessor back on Major Street. It now included print going fuzzy while I tried to decipher the words, familiar objects like apples and oranges suddenly looking strange, as unfamiliar as an exotic piece of Asian fruit. A rambutan. I would surprise myself with not knowing whether I was holding an orange or a grapefruit, a tomato or an apple. Usually, I could sort them out by sniffing or squeezing. As I say, these difficulties were not continuous and static; they changed and changed about. There were times when names came to mind easily, and a few minutes later the right word had vanished. Such confusion came and went. At times I could tell a hawk from a handsaw. My confusions were ingenious: they ranged from not recognizing the names of familiar streets or the well-known titles of books by certain authors to not knowing whether I lived on College Street with my first wife or my second. The faces of friends became separated from their names. Proper nouns of all kinds hovered just out of reach. All this left me shy of entering into a discussion, lest I forget the name of the prime minister or who wrote *Hamlet*.

As I write this, I am reminded that even before my stroke most cars looked alike to me. I hardly ever noticed the colour of a person's eyes or hair. I was blind to such distinctions. Similarly, my lack of interest in sports is almost inhuman. I confuse baseball teams with football clubs now. And I always have. Maybe this is simply a matter of taste and interest. Maybe my stroke hit me in a part of my brain that was never finished in the first place.

A similar vagueness poisoned my grasp of people's names. I don't mean the mild forgetfulness that comes with senior years. I had that, God knows, in spades! This was an added helping of memory loss. Now, and for ever afterwards, I could forget the names of my nearest and dearest. I could forget the names of familiar visitors to my sick room. I might remember the maiden name of my visitor's grandmother, but not the name of the visitor sitting by my bed. Never having had a particularly heavy hand on the vocative, I got away with this more often than I was caught out. And, once I could blame my forgetfulness on my alexia, I could relax about forgetting names and making a mess of a three-way introduction. My affliction let me off the hook I'd been on since high school!

During my early days in hospital, I found that I had a new ability to confuse places. I might walk into my bathroom with the intention of taking a stroll down the corridor, or, worse, walk out into the hallway making preparations to relieve myself. I got confused on the elevator, always forgetting the number of my floor. Once I moved to the rehab hospital, I learned how to cope with a waterlogged memory. I learned to know the right floor by remembering a painting in the corridor opposite the elevator, or remember that my room was on the first floor where one could see a flat rooftop from a window to the left of the elevator. There are hundreds of ways of coping; I discovered a few of them on my own and had help with the others.

Outside my hospital window, the world looked reassuringly the same, although the hospital across the street, the one in which I'd been born, was being slowly demolished. I couldn't fail to connect my presence here with what was going on over there. I saw the irony of that clearly enough. But apart from that, the slow crawl of traffic on University Avenue, the busy demolition workers and their orange machines, helicopters landing on the roof of the Hospital for Sick Children, all reminded me that there was a whole world out there, where getting to work and being on time were serious considerations. My assessment took all of this in, but it omitted the important fact that it was perishingly hot out there. This was summer. And in my air-conditioned cocoon, I'd forgotten.

It was plain that I was no longer playing with fifty-two cards. Although my visitors assured me that on every visit I looked "better than last time," there never was a time when

I'd looked terrible. Not according to friends and relatives, that is. One goes on improving without ever having been badly off. It was a Lewis Carroll world where everything was better and nothing got worse.

Many friends came to visit me. My older children, William and Charlotte; Jacob; Judy, my local sister-in-law and her parents came several times. Old pals from CBC days came, too. Among the most loyal of my visitors was the woman I had been seeing before my stroke, Laura. My stroke occurred when she was in the Middle East on a holiday, which I did not wish to interrupt with the news of my sudden illness. Once she came home, though, she was a constant support and regular visitor.

~

I CAN GIVE YOU ONLY THE SKETCHIEST IDEA of what my daily routine was at Mount Sinai. My subsequent weeks at Toronto Rehab paved over those memories, or so distorted them that I'm no longer sure what took place at the first hospital and what happened at the second. At the same time I was learning more about what memory was and what it could do and what it couldn't. The results of my reflections were a mishmash of conundrums. Keeping to my bed as I did, my world was simplified for me. Like a newborn, I concentrated on simplicity. I ate, I took my medications,

I used the bedpan when the bathroom seemed impossibly far away, and I napped. *Oh, how I napped!*

I didn't quite sleep the clock around, as I might have at home, but I did add considerably to the world's supply of sawn timber. I lost track of time. Each day began with a tidy new slate and it ended about twenty minutes later with my last medications of the day. Time sprinted ahead of me. I had no regrets.

Between visits from friends, family and the professionals, I tried to work out what I was going to do with what was left of my life. I wasn't in a quandary; I wasn't losing it. It was almost like going through an old algebraic formula. The answer would have been a universal truth, not something that applied to me alone. I thought of becoming totally dependent, going into an institution. I thought of the panhandlers on my street, some of whom had become friends. There were some bleak times, certainly. I thought of the title of Caitlan Thomas's memoir of her life after Dylan's death: *Leftover Life to Kill.* Sometimes I seemed to be falling into an enormous pit with a gigantic squid in the water at the bottom. Black times, indeed. But, the funny thing was that these dark moments didn't last.

There is an incident in Ben Hecht's autobiography, *Child of the Century*, where a group of reporters, assigned to write up an execution, bet with one another about whether the condemned man would get up the gallows steps without tripping. They establish a pool, each reporter being assigned one of the thirteen steps leading to the drop. They are certain that the condemned man will stumble and where it happens will make one of their number a lucky police reporter. Later, the prisoner makes monkeys of them all when he climbs the stairs without a stumble. Hecht accounts for this by saying that the betting reporters failed to take into consideration the terminal "high" the condemned man was riding on. It gave him the courage and the strength to make that final climb without faltering. The reporters had forgotten this high, this equivalent to the raptures of the depths that Jacques Cousteau used to talk about in his underwater books.

So it seems that I was a sunny sort of chap while I was in Mount Sinai. Everybody was so nice to me. But I didn't know what I was going to do for a living now that my damaged brain made continuing in my old life quite impossible. I was not indifferent to "the condition my condition was in," but I didn't fret about it. I made a habitation within the reality and tried to make friends with it.

And what was that reality when all is said and done? It wasn't a notice that I was about to lose a leg or an arm. They didn't pass me a note saying that my hearing was gone. My sight was not fading to black. I didn't yet need a "keeper" to wipe my chin and feed me pills twice a day.

What mattered to me was the loss of the ability to read. The idea of being cut off from Shakespeare and company left me weak. My life had been built on reading everything in sight. My jokes were based on reading, my take on current events was informed by reading. I was a one-trick pony, and reading was my trick.

The thought of not reading the comics, billboards and newspaper ads destroyed me. Yet, while I was falling into a depression about my loss, I looked around me and saw people hit far worse than I was by the indiscriminating club of a stroke. We took our pills or gave blood or urine when asked and tried to get through the day.

6

WHEN I LEFT MOUNT SINAI, I was directed to the rehabilitation hospital, which happened to be the next building south on University Avenue. I took my few belongings in a suitcase and a few string bags that seemed to be able to hold all I needed. In addition to this, I brought my *condition*. This condition was and remains a puzzlement, as they say in the song. At times I felt healthy, up to any challenge, the old me. At other times I felt sickly and weak, gone off my Wheaties, more Clark Kent than Superman. This I blamed on my hospitalized state. In any hospital the days all blend together, time slips by noiselessly on rubber wheels. No wonder I felt depleted—I'd had no exercise for weeks.

Okay, I couldn't read either. That bothered me whenever I ran into it.

But there are other things to do in life apart from reading. Most people hardly recognize their literacy. Much of it is almost unconscious: street signs seen out of the corner of the eye, billboards and other advertising, television credits. Hardly the sort of thing Milton defended in his *Areopagitica*.

Besides, I had other, related problems. When I saw faces, I found that I couldn't place them at once. Sometimes, I couldn't place them unless they let slip some clue. Were they relatives or former colleagues? Recognizing faces had become a minor headache: I usually could decipher who they were in a short time, once I could occupy my leftover mind with something other than the problem of putting a name on the person talking to me. This resembled the glitch in the memory of many older people. Everybody, at one time or another, struggles to remember the name of a friend, a movie or a novel. Even Dr. Alzheimer. I had serious problems here. I have a brain full of remembered names but the road out is often blocked with rubble.

I could—or rather, my brain could—accommodate the big blind spot in the upper right quarter of my vision. But when I tried to run my eyes along a line of print in a book or newspaper, I discovered that I now had a blind spot that hid the right-hand side of the line from me. In order to see it, I had to shift my eyes right, along towards the end of the line. By this time in my recovery, though, at least the words no longer looked like they were written in an unfamiliar alphabet. The letters themselves looked like ordinary English letters, not the Serbo-Croatian I had imagined when I felt the first effects of my stroke.

Sometimes the words looked like I was seeing them through a heat haze, as though the light coming off the letters was distorted. Often I would see and read a letter that wasn't in front of me. Habitually, I would read the first letter of the word that came *after* the one I was looking at, so that "director general" might come out "girector general." In both reading the words and in trying to write them down, this last I did with very little trouble. Another visual deficit that now I became aware of was the distortion of familiar objects. The moon, for instance, in whatever phase, looked flat on top. (I haven't checked to see whether the flat part moves to the bottom if I view our satellite from between my legs.)

Geography also mixed me up. In the old days I doted on maps and map reading. Now, I found myself confused in my own neighbourhood. Did Brunswick Street begin at Dupont or Wellesley? Did College intersect with Baldwin, or Ulster with Davenport? All of which I knew before the stroke. Now I sometimes forget the name of the street I live on. This is also true of those smaller geographies one runs into. In the kitchen: where do the can-openers go? Where are the clean dishtowels kept? When I first returned home from the Rehab, I kept finding cans of tuna in the dishwasher and jars of pencils in the freezer. Luckily, such mistakes were easy to correct.

I was moved out of Mount Sinai on August 7, 2001, after a stay of a week. My memory of the actual passage of time is primitive at best. I retain a few impressions, vistas and meetings with visitors, but not much with which to patch a torn memory. To indicate how vague I was about time in those days, let me quote from my journal:

> I was only in Mount Sinai for a short time, about two weeks. Then I was moved south on University Avenue to the Toronto Rehabilitation Hospital. It was the hospital next door. I could have made the transfer myself, without help, but, of course, I had all I needed. At some point I was wheeled through an underground tunnel. I think that was to Toronto General for some tests. It's confused in my mind. But confusion isn't amnesia, I hadn't lost my memory, simply mislaid it.

My recollections of this institution are firmer and clearer than those of my stay at Mount Sinai. I was at the Rehab longer, for one thing, and I was recovering. In the words of the old cliché, every day in every way I was getting better and better. But the vault of my memory still had holes in it.

~

I BECAME AWARE that one nurse seemed to be with me more often than any of the others. Her name was Kathy Nelson. I held on to the name by fixing the first name with a thought of Heathcliff's great love, Catherine Earnshaw, in *Wuthering Heights*. Her last name I associated with the heroic Horatio Nelson of the Royal Navy. A peculiar and complicated device, but it worked most of the time, although I sometimes had to run through a long list of seafaring men from Horatio Hornblower and Peter Blood to Captain Bligh and Fletcher Christian. Even after the years that have passed since I first met Kathy Nelson, I sometimes still have to go through my old mnemonic strategy. I use the method for recalling almost everybody's name. If I don't set up some sort of trick to recall a name, it would get lost in the limbo of the mislaid and forgotten, only to be dredged up when I was looking for something else.

One doctor had an old Puritan name, like Godbehere or Meanwell or Come-as-you-are. Another doctor had a Prussian last name fitted to a very North American first name. There were other doctors, too, but they seemed to always be on their way somewhere else. Unlike the nursing staff, they didn't abide. They "looked in" on me, as though I were a footnote that might be skipped if lack of time were a concern.

I got to know the different shifts the staff worked and looked forward to the return of Kathy Nelson's shift. I appreciated getting straight answers from her. I became attached to Kathy. I regarded her as *my* nurse. *Mine.*

There were other professionals on the floor, too, of course, but they were not as personally mine as I imagined Kathy to be. They looked in on me, introduced me to the routine, got me moving again. As I discovered, a person in my condition had no real business staying in bed. I was not sick. A little weak at the knees, maybe, but not sick. I didn't require peace, calm and bedrest. No, in hospitals, the keeping of a patient in bed is mostly a matter of filing. They kept you where they could find you. And it was effective.

After the first couple of days, I was encouraged to get out of bed and take my meals in the dining room with most of the other patients. I found out that this floor—I was uncertain which floor it was—was devoted to brain injuries. Most of us were stroke victims. *Stroke survivors*, they called us. The patients who were not confined to their beds moved about with canes, crutches and wheelchairs. The dining room was opposite the nursing station. A large sign was posted outside the dining room. It told us the day of the week, the month and even the year. It was very useful, and the size of the words and numbers reassured us all that we were back on the road to good health.

The sunlight coming in the windows along the east side of the dining room made this an attractive place to have a meal. There was a TV going at the far end of the room, but only the die-hard TV junkies watched it. I found myself eating with a group of men who were recovering from strokes that had brought them here from all over. Three at my table were originally from Belgium and loved to talk about the great restaurants they had dined at in Europe and Asia. One was an engineer, another a banker, the third an architect, I think. There was a former diplomat, too, who enjoyed talking to the Belgians, although he was from farther east of Belgium, somewhere in the Balkans. He was soft-spoken, cultured and always helpful to me and the rest of the regular gang sitting at the table. He knew what to do with Swiss francs in a falling market, and had wonderful stories about our better-known diplomats. He had first become acquainted with Canada during a diplomatic posting here. Later, when things had changed in his native country, he came to Canada permanently.

Sitting with the gourmets and listening to their talk of gourmet meals in far-off places tended to make one forget where we were in fact. It was reassuring to hear about a little hole-in-the-wall café around the corner from the

Paris Opéra. I had done a share of foreign travel as well and added my own stories of memorable meals on the Seine or Loire, at the harbour at Kyrenia and Famagusta and in pubs along the Thames. To me it was more reassuring than their talk of the unstable franc and the fluctuating dollar. That was when I felt like an amateur. They had been everywhere and seen everything, while I had hardly wet my paddle in salt water. When I entered the conversation it was to make a local point, or to draw on my experiences in Paris, London and Nicosia. In my own gang, I could pass as well travelled, but not here.

At the table, our foreign travels made us all companions and equals. But once away from the table, we were again stroke victims: some of us being pushed in our wheelchairs by friends who needed crutches to move along the corridor. We helped one another out in small ways, like moving a chair away from the table so that a wheelchair might take its place.

I noticed a woman who talked back to the faces on the TV screen. She was wistful when talking to a fellow patient, but a loud and opinionated critic when it came to the television. She ordered faces off the set, called smiling hosts imbeciles, and did this in a strong, affirmative voice. The television set was her enemy and she addressed it as such, but in another sense, it was her companion in this ward of strangers. Another patient was a lovely woman who had been in the stroke unit before. This made her a celebrity, someone we all looked up to. She was able to explain the drill to the rest of us and set us right about the rumours that we were starting based upon little information. Her strength and good humour sustained the rest of us.

The food, when I first tasted it, was fine. I was soon told by patients who had been there longer than I had that the longer I stayed there, the closer I came to my release date, the worse the food would get. And it was true. My opinion of the food did alter. It was a sign of our readiness to be returned to the *world-out-there* when we found that the food was terrible. Of course, I knew nothing of this at the time, although I often suspected that the meat and the gravy met for the first time on my plate.

But while the meals would never excite the compilers of the *Guide Michelin*, they were tolerable, and mealtimes were the benchmarks of our days. Getting to and from the dining room helped us to measure our progress. Early on, I got to the table exhausted and then back to my bed ready to collapse. Bedrest had made a rag doll of me. I needed to get some exercise to get my body back in shape.

The thought was father to the deed. Early on I was told that there was a gym downstairs and that I was expected to spend some time every day getting myself back in shape. I had never been a healthy specimen to begin with. I never had done any exercise. I was the ninety-eight-pound weakling who had never gambled a stamp to send for Charles Atlas's Dynamic Tension system of body-building. I had learned to live with getting sand kicked in my face at the beach. Still, in this gym, I was surprised to see that some of the people working out had been in great shape when their strokes side-lined them. Like the old medieval figure of Death, strokes were no respecters of physique or education. We were all lev-elled by the sweep of its swinging blade.

The gym was well organized, not for group activities but for individual assessment and work. Staff therapists worked with the patients, helping them to strengthen stroke-weakened limbs. Some patients were trying to lift an arm or leg, some were practising walking up and down a flight of stairs. There was a certain solemnity about it, not quite the raucous din of an ordinary gym. People don't like to look their infirmities in the eye, even with a helpful therapist ready to lend a hand. But I watched patients work at their problems and even smile at minor breakthroughs: an arm that couldn't bend *this* far yesterday or the day before; legs that wouldn't sup-port the weight of a body, now managing with two canes or a metal walker.

On my first day, I was timed to see how long it took me to walk down the hall. I don't know whether they were test-ing my heart, my powers of locomotion or my shortness of breath. The test was repeated at intervals. I guess that was a measure of my improvements. It also kept me busy until the treadmills were free.

They put me to work on a treadmill that had electronically built-in hills and rough places. A stationary bicycle provided my legs with the electronic equivalent of a hike in rough country. I was also set to work scrambling over an uncertain suspended walkway. Although it was less than an inch from the floor, it had the sway and pitch of a suspended rope bridge high up in an Asian jungle with the river running swiftly over jagged rocks a hundred metres below. I had to keep my wits about me to maintain myself upright. I was also set to climbing the stairs.

The therapist in charge had a cheerful voice and a colourful turn of phrase, a gift for vivid descriptions. I looked forward to our sessions, even though I realized that most of her patients were struggling with their acquired infirmities more than I was. While I jogged on the spot, they were stretching to reach her hand, attempting to bend a knee. I was struck by the way this therapist found the right encouraging words. She should try writing a book one day.

I was treated to the gym two or three times a week. I recall going down there often, but my mind failed to take note of when I went. It was probably every Monday, Wednesday and Friday or every Tuesday and Thursday. I remember that repetition occurred, but forgot the details. The frequency of the repetition did me in every time. All dates and appointments were random; they had no sticking power in my brain. I have no idea of frequency. Just as finding my way to and from the gym posed problems for my poor mind, so did patterns of frequency. My mind had stopped noticing such things. Those wires had been pulled. Every appointment seemed random, ad hoc, lacking the logic of a simple order and design. I seemed to have lost the ability to recognize recurrence. Unless a nurse reminded me, I missed my appointments. Still today, I don't get around to doing things like returning telephone calls, sorting through my mail and completing my income tax.

I have been wondering whether some of this might not have been present *before* my stroke as a peculiarity of my particular brain. I don't mean to imply that I have always mixed up dates and appointments, and forgotten to return messages, but rather that the frequency of an occurrence is not the most fixed feature of my brain. For instance, as I mentioned earlier, I recall finding among my parents' books a few in which my childish self drew pictures of steam locomotives on the fly-leaves. As the work of a three- or four-year-old they were never great art, but they did record something of the same difficulty that has plagued me since my time in the Rehab. The drawings showed that over the back fence I had taken in most of the main features of a locomotive running down the Canadian National tracks to the station. The interesting feature is this: while I showed the smokestack and bell on top of the engine, and the coal car and the right-angle bend that indicated the cab for the fireman and engineer, I totally missed the number of rounded bumps along the top of the old locomotive. My drawing exaggerated the normal one or two bumps to a line of six or more, so that the sketch looked rather like an up-ended nursing sow. I had failed to grasp the number of bumps, although I had hit on the idea of "bumpishness." Similarly, although I had grasped the idea that the train's wheels came in pairs, one on each side, I totally missed the idea of how many sets of wheels might be attached. I got part of the reality, but failed to take in the numerical part of it. Perhaps I'm making more of this than I should; numeracy is not well developed in all four-year-olds.

~

THE GEOGRAPHY OF THE HOSPITAL buffaloed me once I had to make my way from one appointment to another, all on different floors. I had been shown how to avoid locked doors on some floors, by using other banks of elevators. I learned to recognize one therapist's office, not by the room number or the floor or the distance from the elevator but by the painting hanging in the hall beside her door. I learned to recognize my own floor by the way the light filled the hall just opposite the elevator. My floor was the first level above an added wing, and the natural light on the fifth floor couldn't be confused with the electric light that lit the floors below.

So, I was made aware that I had lost some of my customary methods of navigation. I no longer *knew* where things were without thinking. I had to blaze trails through an unfamiliar bush. Some, perhaps most, of these blazes stayed with me, and I walked the corridors with something approaching assurance. But a handful of destinations always eluded my schemes and stratagems. My own floor was one of these. Without paying attention to the quality of light in the hall, I would get lost three or four times a day. My floor number wouldn't stay with me. It seemed to be a random number and it got lost among all the other numbers it might possibly have been. I couldn't make it stick in my head. It was gone as fast as the name of someone introduced at a cocktail party. Faster.

I learned to live without a daily newspaper. I became addicted to my radio. I made meetings with friends an opportunity to catch up on the news of the day. I doted on lively debates and discussions because I was no longer getting them through print. But I picked up new habits the way photographers today get used to holding the camera away from their faces. Only small adjustments are required.

Gradually, I got the hang of the way my brain was working now. It did most of what I wanted it to do, but it had sand traps that I learned to avoid. I knew I could no longer rely on the "sticking plaster" of memory. I could forget a word in the second part of what I was saying, even though I had already used the word a moment earlier. I could no longer depend on being able to say what I had in my mind. I had to work my way through what I had on my mind to say before I said it. And when an idea for additional information to throw into a discussion came into my head, it often evaporated when I was on the point of saying it. This obstacle turned me into more of a listener than a talker, which gave my friends some relief.

I learned to write things down in the "memory book" that was given to me in the rehab hospital. It was a simple three-ring binder, the sort high-school girls clutch to their young bosoms as they march from class to class. My nurse, Kathy Nelson, explained to me that I should write down the times of my appointments on its blue-lined pages, use it to get down phone numbers and directions to get me to the gym and to the reading clinic. She told me to make friends with my memory book because it was going to become an important ally in keeping me sane and the hospital services on schedule. I wrote my name in it, surprising myself that my fingers could still form the letters for my pencil. The memory book gave a lift to my sense of being in the driver's seat of my life. The binder became my constant companion: part diary, part

If this is my __Memory Book__, it hasn't
been doing a very good job. Or I
haven't. It hides in pockets &
drawers & stays out of sight. It's
never around when you need it.

I'll try again. Now it's June '04.
Yesterday was the 100th anniversary
of "Bloomsday." I went to help
celebrate the republication of
most of Morley Callaghan's stories.
I would have thought that Bob
Weaver would have been there, but
he wasn't. I wouldn't have gone
either, had not Don Summerhayes
told me about it & offered me
a lift with Marlin Homer, his
curiously named wife. (who
is lovely & charming.)

Barry made a good show of it at
Harbourfront, with a dixieland
band & 4 writers who spoke:
Anne Michaels, André Alexis, &
Alistair MacLeod & Margaret Atwood

appointment book, part commonplace book. Hospitals, to a degree, I think, breed a passive spirit; the memory book returned a piece of myself to me. I learned to write down not only the name of the person just introduced but to scribble some special fact that might make the new name leap out from all the others, so that my book was filled with notes like this:

George Dalton: friend of Susan, from the bookstore
  or
Mary Bett: Michael's sister, from St. Catharines.

I was taking my days one at a time. I lacked the nerve to look down the barrel of what was to come. I had already started imagining my writing career as something in my past. How could I look at it otherwise? At the same time, I wasn't looking for other things to do. I was living with the future a perfect vacuum. I didn't worry about feeding Jacob, preparing my income tax forms or paying my monthly utility bills. Unknown to me, my oldest son, William, was looking after these practical considerations.

I could remember everything, except when I needed it. Even now, some years after all of this was new to me, I am frequently in conversation with people I know well but whose names forever escape me. They lack the adhesive quality that used to fix things in my head. As I said earlier, I was never a man with a heavy foot on the vocative. I didn't sprinkle the names of the persons addressed through my conversations with them. Now, of course, I skip names, not out of disrespect or rudeness but of necessity. Faces I remembered well enough, but names were off in a far country.

~

I'VE MENTIONED TESTS, but, as far as I remember, I haven't given any samples of the sort of things I was exposed to. One kind of problem read like this:

Sam received a red bike for his birthday. The present made him feel
a) cold b) happy c) afraid d) sad

Betty snapped the book shut. The story was about a horse, and she did not like
a) animal stories b) history c) adventure stories
d) people

And so on. I knew that Sam might feel *happy* about the new bike, but I suppose there are some boys who might have a different reaction to the intrusive challenge of a new bike. Although I didn't answer *afraid* or *sad*, I was tempted.

When read with any imagination at all, a writer like me could end up scoring zero on such a test.

Another test had me add a single letter to make a word out of a group of letters with a dash somewhere among them. I added an "a" to "gl—ss" and an "s" to "pla—tic," but "—atch" confused me. I didn't know whether they wanted "batch," "patch," "latch," "watch," "hatch," "match" or "catch." So I put them all in.

Once I had broken the code of what the instructions wanted me to do, I usually had no difficulty in making a "normal" response. In tests of memory itself, I failed horribly: I couldn't list the names of a dozen objects left on a tray for me to examine for thirty seconds until they were covered or removed. I was given the usual IQ tests, which gave me little trouble, but tests that required me to retain information or repeat new information got the better of me.

These tests were given to me by specialized social workers. We met for a period of several hours stretched over a couple of weeks. In the department's small kitchen, one group got me to try my hand at cooking. I made breakfast and heated canned soup. Another team of social workers took me out of the safe environment of the Rehab and cast me away on the city streets, following my progress at a distance as I accepted the challenges of streetcars, buses and the subway. They watched as I paid my fare or dug in my pockets for tickets or tokens. They stood by while I negotiated with ticket sellers or worked out a route on a posted map of the transit system.

Meanwhile, every day I worked with a reading specialist. The exercises went beyond simple reading of texts and brought me into a review of the streets of my neighbourhood and the names of familiar things like bookstores and restaurants, where I spend far more time than I can afford.

Forcing myself to decipher the letters on signs all around me helped strengthen my reading. As time went on, I improved my navigation through the city.

At my side throughout this period was a team of doctors and nurses. In addition, I saw several specialists in several kinds of rehabilitation. One tended to my body. No use having a healthy mind if you have no healthy place to put it. Others watched over my movements as I rediscovered the joys of public transportation, relearned the mysteries of the supermarket and the kitchen. Porters led me about the hospital from one department to another. Then, when I had had my X-ray or dental examination or had seen another specialist, they took me back to my room, until I learned to navigate myself.

After a time, my keepers untied the strings and let me go about on my own, taking public transportation or a walk down the aisles at the supermarket as the mood took me.

In all of these activities, I felt as self-conscious as a fraternity pledge: over-eager to get things right, and consequently making uncharacteristic errors and getting into muddles. I found I couldn't distinguish the signs inside the subway: what does "upbound" mean? What is the exact fare? Do I need a transfer or not? Habit and familiarity helped me out when I got confused. A few times I missed my station.

Similarly, in the kitchen, reading directions from the cookbook was still too much for me, so I stayed away from printed information. This happened when I was looking at an aisle of soup cans at the market. So many of the soup and fish cans looked alike. I had to pause to make sure that the tuna in my hand wasn't really salmon or anchovies, or that they weren't swimming in a tomato sauce. Time after time, confusion won out over my best precautions. I bought items I thought were something else. I wandered around the store without any sense of where things were, how similar items were to be found on adjacent racks. As my lists were made up of items as I thought of them, I wastefully criss-crossed the store rather than picking up all the similar things at the same time. I'm sure that my path through the store must have looked like the route of a drugged rat through a maze. I missed the bargains as well as the temptations. My helpers followed my progress in the supermarket as I tried to remember the items I needed to buy. Later on they watched me cook a lunch in the department's tiny kitchen. They saw that I could still make an omelette and fried potatoes. I didn't try anything complicated; this was no time for *cassoulet, vichyssoise* or *rognons de boeuf.* Like a young bride, I wanted no failures.

~

BACK AT THE REHAB, I spent an hour or more three times a week with Lea Ayuyao, the speech-language pathologist, addressing my reading difficulties directly. Lea told Barbara Meissner Fishbein, who writes for *CASLPO Today* (College of Audiologists and Speech-Language Pathologists of Ontario), that I impressed her with my description of a picture she presented to me. Of course, I remember nothing of the incident myself. Much later, after I returned home, I learned of her assessment of our meeting in the magazine's pages.

"It was then that I knew Howard was no ordinary patient," she was quoted as saying in the article about my alexia. "His writing was much more detailed and descriptive than [that of] any other patient I had ever seen." In the first session, Lea began to explore my deficits. She admitted that this was a rare opportunity to explore what remained of my brain. "We don't usually see such discrete disorders of reading with writing intact, but more importantly, in a patient with such superior communication skills. He could describe exactly what processes he was using to decode written material." Barbara Fishbein went on to remark, "In working with Engel, Ayuyao realized that he was giving her a unique window into his deficit. They became true partners in working toward improving his function."

As I read the above, I try to remember that it is me that both Lea and Barbara are describing. At this distance, memory has worn thin, and I have to cram my way into that awkward past, trying neither to romanticize it nor insert easy historical links that are the invention of the writer in me. For instance, I don't recall if at that time I was thinking about whether I was going to continue writing. I have no idea that I had decided to give it up either. One of my therapists, Marla Roth, discussed with me what sort of thing I might try to do in a new work of fiction. I pondered the question and, more than once, almost gave it up as a pipe dream. After all, I couldn't even read a daily newspaper. I couldn't hold an idea in my head for more than a moment.

I don't, honestly, remember what I was thinking about in those days. This was true about most aspects of my life. Was I going to return to Major Street? Was I going to change all of my old habits? Now, as an illiterate, was I going to be able to continue as a member of the Senior Common Room at University College, or Massey College in the University of Toronto? Was I going to be able to rejoin my cronies at Quotes or Dooney's for lunch? Perhaps I just wasn't thinking about the future, giving myself some space to consider it later on. At Scarlett O'Hara's beloved plantation, Tara, maybe, where thinking is best left for tomorrow.

~

ON THE SUGGESTION OF A THERAPIST at the Rehab, I started seeing Michelle Cohen, a transplanted South African who has been working with people exhibiting difficulties similar to mine for many years. We met in her home in north Toronto, where she had set up a powerful battery of computers. Although the space was small, there seemed to be room for everything. I met with her from February fairly frequently until May 2002, and then less often during June and July. She remembers that it took me five minutes to read eighteen short lines, where the average person would have read the 465 words, about forty-five lines, in half that time.

As a "letter by letter" reader I might get through one or two lines in the same time as it took others to read a whole page. In spite of my snail's pace, my reading was one hundred percent accurate. But I was not able to scan a page, and the whole process was exhausting beyond belief.

I remember that the passage I read was a short biography of the World War I spy Mata Hari. Each time I took up the book, I read a little further, and each time brought poor Mata closer to her rendezvous with the French firing squad in the park at Vincennes, on the outskirts of Paris. I think we stopped reading before the fatal volley. Michelle could show me how I had improved over the weeks and weeks we had been working together. Using the computer, she was able to flash up three, four and up to seven-letter words for two or three seconds each, and decrease the exposure time until my response time improved to one second. With longer words, up to seven letters, I was not able to improve my time by much. This technique, which I mentioned earlier, reminds me of Kim's Game. In the Rudyard Kipling novel *Kim*, the boy hero is introduced to the game of recognizing unrelated objects exposed for a limited time on a tray. When the tray has been covered, the boy is asked to recall in detail the objects he has seen. All of this was to train him for the work of a spy for the British Raj. With the advent of the computer, this recognition and memory game has been shot into another orbit.

Michelle tried to help me to examine words or sentences at their beginning, middle and end, but to no avail: my letter-by-letter reading continued to plague me. Words of different lengths, like *cat*, *table* and *hippopotamus*, are processed in my head at a different rate. Each added letter adds more weight to the load that I am trying to lift.

Michelle developed, or had developed for her, a computer program that I could control. It fed me words of a chosen length for me to identify in a given time. I was able to take this program home with me. She encouraged me to try "whole word" reading, which I did. On my own, I remember reading a short passage about Ernest Hemingway. Every time his name appeared in the short account of one of his adventures, I sounded out his name again and again and again. By the time I had finished a column of the story, I was angry at myself. I felt stupid, as though I had suddenly discovered that you can't buy shoes in a liquor store, or beer at the library. But there was improvement: my reading rate increased to thirty-five words per minute from twenty-five.

In 2005, Michelle Cohen told the journalist Barbara Meissner Fishbein: "What made Engel unique was his willingness to embrace strategies, accept his deficits, and go about accomplishing his goals in a different way. He was delightful to work with and so very appreciative."

I should add, at this point, that I was impressed by the skill, dedication and inventiveness of all the therapists I worked with, both in the Rehab and, later, when I was back on the street. What I learned from them I quickly absorbed and made use of, and I used much of it again to buttress the authenticity of the novel I had started working on.

They had dropped the coloured stones that I followed to discover the way out of the forest. For this alone, I am forever in their debt.

7

THE PROBLEMS NEVER WENT AWAY, but I became cleverer at solving them. One thing I learned that was very useful: I tried to eliminate the unnecessary distractions from what I was doing, cut down on the noisy confusions by concentrating on the object of whatever quest I was on.

When the therapists first took me out of the hospital, I was shocked at the heat of the streets. I had taken the air-conditioned rooms and halls of the hospital as the norm of a summer afternoon in the city. Another thing that bothered me was the noise. Street noise seemed to be a sort of mental confusion, as though noise itself was confusion.

My own self-absorption did not prevent my sympathetic response to others. I listened to the conversations of

my roommate with his wife about the problems of building a wheelchair-friendly ramp that led from the car to the
house, or my concern for the health of my earlier roommate's wife, who seemed to be coping with her husband's
difficulties less well than he was. Whenever she came, her
face betrayed her confusion.

One thing surprised me when I began to inspect the
diary I kept in hospital. I remember staring out the window of my room and down into the streets as though I had
never walked those streets or driven a car along them. In
fact, I discovered that my access to those streets has been
unobstructed. I went out many times. I joined friends for
lunch south of the hospital, on King Street, and met others at a café near my house off Bloor Street. My presence
shocked the regulars, who knew where I was spending my
nights, but they quickly overcame their surprise—which
was really only a filing disorder. They had placed me in
the hospital: what was I doing at my favourite luncheon
spots? But that wasn't my problem. Mine was the impression of a long and uninterrupted hospital stay. Which was
not the reality.

Another reality that became evident only when I began
looking for it some time later was the fact that I really never
stopped writing. I kept up my memory book, making
entries of doctors' appointments and trips to my various
therapists. I kept up my diary almost from the first. The

fact that I couldn't read hadn't stopped me from writing. That my memory of what I had written was feeble didn't stop me from putting more detailed notes about the day's events into words. At times the handwriting was erratic: no two pages looked as though they had been penned by the same hand. So, while I was thinking that I might never successfully put pen to paper again, I was keeping in daily practice.

At first, I had no thoughts of writing a book. That was not only well beyond my abilities, it was also beyond my imagination. But without my knowing it, another part of my brain was beginning to plot out a story. Images began popping into my head. Plots and plot twists began haunting my imagination. While I was lying in my hospital bed, having another of those long naps I had become addicted to, I was hard at work inventing story and characters and situations for the book I still didn't know I was writing.

8

EXAMINING THE PROCESS NOW, I don't know when I moved away from feeling that I was a former writer, the literary equivalent of Monty Python's dead parrot. I think I was partly sheltered from the impact by the alexia itself: what I couldn't see didn't exist to a degree, and where I was aware of a problem, my sunny post-recovery euphoria carried me along, not worrying my head with such practical matters as what was I going to do with my leftover days. In the hospital I was being told that while I couldn't read, I could still write. At the time, this was cold comfort. It was like being given permission to tap dance all the way to the scaffold. I didn't think in terms of going on with my writer's life any more than I imagined any other aspect of my pre-stroke life.

In spite of this largely unnoticed dark cloud hanging over me, I got on with my therapists and jumped through all their hoops when asked without much thought about how I was intending to put food on the table and keep up the mortgage payments. I remember wondering why some kind anonymous soul had sent me a cheque for a considerable amount of money. I was a junkie, so high that I didn't understand why the firemen had come after me on a burning rooftop. That's how confused I was as they prepared me for the working world again.

On other matters I was reasonably well organized. I didn't act as though half of my brain was having a nap. I looked and acted like the old me. I could tell you who directed *Citizen Kane* and *Rio Bravo*, or who wrote *Pride and Prejudice* and *Measure for Measure*. My handwriting still didn't resemble what I remembered as my own, but others could read it and even I could make sense of most of my jottings. In fact, I made endless notes to myself, most of which I copied at least once, because the newest version was easier to read than the older one. In a typical note to myself, I might record the date or time of an event twice on the same scrap of paper. And I got used to having an obscured field of vision; most of the time I didn't notice it.

My store of anecdotes remained intact: I could still bore friends by telling the same old story again and again, like a normal person. I could still quote Shakespeare and other writers when it seemed to fit into the conversation. I could answer my friends' questions about Robertson Davies, John Ford or Ernest Hemingway. I could still tie my own shoes and remember that Christmas wasn't celebrated in July. I could distinguish between Zeus and Dr. Seuss. I could even stand up in front of a room full of people and be trusted not to make a complete ass of myself mistaking the Canada Council for the local rate-payers' association. I was doing well. No mistake. But writing was another matter.

I was comfortable in the Rehab. I wandered the corridors, talked to my fellow patients and had been given leave to help myself to coffee in the nurses' kitchen. By now there wasn't a face on the floor I wasn't familiar with. I had the run of the place. Some of the staff were even reading my books. No wonder I was happy there and gave little thought to going home.

On the suggestion of one of my therapists, Marla Roth, I wrote a letter to Dr. Oliver Sacks, a neurologist in New York City. Marla and I had been discussing my problems and comparing them with those of the patients who figure in Sacks's well-known book *The Man Who Mistook His Wife for a Hat*. We discussed his other writings, too: *A Leg to Stand On*, which shows Sacks's struggle with a misbehaving limb after a climbing accident; the memorable case of the people who were miraculously but temporarily healed by L-Dopa in his book *Awakenings*. I was delighted to have had the chance to compare my own case with those discussed by the noted neurologist, for it struck me that my situation was peculiar for a writer and I was glad to find that someone else agreed. (Earlier in my hospital stay, I was surprised to find that the head of the department had never heard of Sacks or his books.) Together Marla and I thought that "The Writer Who Could Not Read" might not be out of place in a future work. So, with Marla's encouragement, I wrote my letter.

That was early in 2002, as close as I can figure it now. I tried keeping track of important dates. When I had my stroke, when I moved from one hospital to another, when I was discharged and when I saw the last of the therapists who followed me home to sort out domestic matters: all important dates, but, alas, most of them have been winnowed away by my imperfect note-taking and general fecklessness.

A week or so later, I received a polite reply to my letter. Dr. Sacks commented on what I had said and wished me well. His letter addressed the issues I mentioned, but his signature at the end of the page did not promise or suggest further correspondence. This, when I thought about it, was what I should have expected. A busy medical practitioner and writer cannot enter into correspondence with everybody who thinks he has a unique condition. I felt I was lucky to have received so speedy and sympathetic a response.

Having put Dr. Sacks out of my mind, I got on with other things: running up and down the stairs in the gym, pedalling the stationary bicycle and chatting up my fellow patients and nurses. A few days later, I received a second letter from New York. In it, Dr. Sacks wanted my permission to quote from my first letter in an article he was preparing for *The New Yorker* magazine. As an assiduous and long-time reader of that magazine, and someone still in awe of this second letter, I fired off an immediate reply, giving him permission to quote what he liked. His next letter contained a pre-publication printout of his article along with the invitation to call him whenever I happened to be in Manhattan.

The article appeared in *The New Yorker* on October 7, 2002, with Oliver Sacks's byline and under the headings:

A Neurologist's Notebook
The Case of Anna H.
Why was she losing her ability to recognize familiar objects by sight?

A page and a half into the article, he quoted what I had written in my letter:

An ability to write despite an alexia is not that uncommon. I recently received a letter from Howard Engel, a Canadian novelist, who told me that he had a somewhat similar problem following a stroke. "The area affected," he relates, "was my ability to read. I can write, but I can't read what I've just written . . . So, I can write, but I can't rewrite . . . My vision for the most part is unaffected until I look at a text. Then, whatever I'm looking at turns into unfamiliar blocks of type that could at first glance be taken for Serbo-Croatian. Familiar words, including my own name, are unfamiliar blocks of type and have to be sounded out slowly. Each time a name recurs in an article or review, it hits me as unfamiliar on its last appearance as it does on the first.

I can't deny that I was delighted to see myself quoted in *The New Yorker*. Years ago I used to send the magazines cartoons, which were returned to me with rejection slips. This happened often enough for me to think that an elastic was attached to my submission even as I dropped it into the letterbox. And I had followed the careers and fortunes of the magazine's luminaries, like Thurber, Ross, Shawn and the Whites, for decades. I remember a party in a third-floor walk-up overlooking the Seine in the Paris of the 1960s when a drinking friend of mine had a story accepted by the magazine. My good friend Eric Wright had a story printed in the magazine. As far as I was concerned, and most writers agree with this, *The New Yorker* is the best magazine, the best home for a story.

Well, I didn't have a story. I'd had an honourable mention in Oliver Sacks's story. What I wanted to do was get out of the hospital, back to my computer and start giving myself a chance to get into the magazine by my own efforts. In this resolve, the magazine was simply a symbol of all the writing I now hoped to do.

At the same time, I was spending more and more time outside the institution: weekends at home, lunches with my cronies, meetings with friends. But the shot was clearly on the table: I was being groomed for discharge. The therapists redoubled their efforts. I was given another chance to confuse oranges and apples. My reading therapist helped me to recall the names of the streets near my home. I was driven there to check out the place while William and Jacob, my sons, who had been managing in my absence, looked on. The hospital still had claims on me; I wasn't being turned loose yet, but simply being given an airing on my old street and a chance to see where I used to live, and where I would eventually return.

9

I'M TRYING TO REMEMBER when I finally cut my umbilicus to the Rehab. I think I recall a drive in a car, perhaps with Laura, and seeing familiar buildings on unfamiliar corners. Every vista was like a test in some game: "What's wrong with this picture?" It wasn't quite like the old Simon-Binet cards that showed firemen busy having their lunch while fire raged in the house beside them. Nor did I see raccoons and ducks in the trees while fish and puppies scampered on the grass. The world looked rational enough. Perhaps the effect on me is best described by comparing my drive home to a drive made after a twenty-year absence, not fourteen weeks.

I know that my son William had seen to it that the house was clean, that the bed was fresh, that the laundry was crisp in the proper drawers and closets. But I brought my own baggage of confusion with me. I know that what had appeared to me to have been an unbroken term at the Rehab had in fact been a stretch of time punctuated with almost daily excursions into the outside world. I had even made a visit home with two of my occupational therapists. I showed them around, but recall little else of this visit.

The note in my diary, written at the time I left University Avenue, reads:

LAST DAY AT REHAB. Last taste of 5th Floor East at 550 University. Said goodbye to nurses and a few patients. Lunch at Italian place on Eglinton. All of us had a bad reaction from the food. Bad night for Will, Laura and me. Good to be in my own bed, although I'm spooked by the clutter in the house . . . Slept well and long. Was very tired.

The move back home must have occurred in Laura's car. In my memory, Jacob doesn't seem to be on the scene. If the move was accomplished during the day, then Jacob was still in school. My reaction to what I saw as clutter was very likely my reaction to accumulated read and unread newspapers and magazines. I remember that they seemed to assault me. I stopped delivery soon after this; I needed

Oct

Tue 2 <u>LAST DAY AT REHAB</u>

Last taste of 5th Floor East @ 550 University. Said goodbye to nurses + a few patients. Lunch at Italian place on Eglinton. All of us had a bad reaction from the Joy. Bad nights for Will, Laura & me. Good to be in my own bed, although I'm spooked by the clutter in the house. It's like Pass moved back into my life. Slept well & long. Was very tired.

Wed 3 Well, I woke up in my own bed again. A was there + as soon too was Jacob. Alice had been making a fuss since dawn & continued until she had the room to herself. Will made me breakfast + I walked to Bathurst St & then to Doonie's for coffee + to hear the chat of the regulars. Sorted through my pills looking for "live" one. Will home. Book arrived from NY. Why, I don't know.

Thurs 4 Again, I woke in my own bed. Will got a call that his house in Kingston had been robbed + so he headed off there in my car. Rosemary Kelly took me to Mount Sinai for a Cat Scan. We had lunch + walked back to Major St running into J on route. Will made dinner for J + Kelly + me. Will + Kelly headed off to move heavy items for Kelly. My new frustrates me at every turn. I walked a good deal + but still feel cat-weak. Almost any conversation gets to be too complicated for me.

Fri 5 Jay + Sue

I think I napped a lot, fighting a cold + reacting to the realities of looming war + retaliation in the Middle East. Frustrated in not having more control of my life + my surroundings. It's good to be with J + Will again. Reading still the basic frustration of my life. It turns up everywhere.

a calm place; newsprint was noisy and unsettling in a way that books were not. Not then, not ever.

The next day I began making adjustments. There were no nurses checking up on me. My bodily fluids were my own again. I began to adapt myself.

> Well, I woke up in my own bed. Laura was there, and so, too, was Jacob. Alice [the cat] had been making a fuss since dawn, and continued until she had the room to herself. William made me breakfast. I walked to Bathurst Street and then to Dooney's for coffee and to hear the chat of the regulars. Sorted through my pens looking for a "live" one . . . Book arrived from New York. Why, I don't know.

Slowly, I made my adjustments to civilian life after my skirmishes with the medical world on University Avenue. My head was not totally free of confusion. I caught myself putting the leftovers in the garbage and the garbage in the dishwasher a few times. I found some laundry in there as well. But these lapses are mostly self-correcting: a second glance finds the error, which is easily put right.

I wasn't free of the hospital completely. Tendrils of the medical system followed me home. I had to return to have a CAT scan, and therapists turned up regularly to show me the difference between mustard and mayonnaise, and to help me organize my bill-paying routine. At some point, William had to return to his house in the country because it had been vandalized in his absence. In his place, friends like Rosemary Kelly and Ann Barnette came to my rescue. They took me back into the hospitals for tests, X-rays and scans, and brought me home again.

> My new head frustrates me at every turn. Almost every conversation gets to be too complicated for me ... Frustrated in not having more control of my life and my surroundings ... It's good to be with Jacob and Will again. Reading is still the basic frustration of my life. It turns up everywhere ... I went with Judy [my sister-in-law] on a guided tour of Mount Pleasant Cemetery's notable landmarks.

By now I was going out to have family dinners at Judy's or the Hamilton's on weekends. My in-laws were a great bastion of support for us at this time. Arthur and Doris Hamilton always included Jacob and me in family reunions, when Janet's brother, Jay, and sister, Mary, came from Edmonton to see their sister Judy and their parents in north Toronto, and before that in Kleinberg. Arthur was a United Church minister who had worked his way east one parish at a time. He and Doris had been pioneers in the Peace River country early in their marriage. An all-around sportsman and gardener, Arthur had always been a second father to me, and both my in-laws gave me abundant support when I became, at the death of their daughter Janet, a single parent. Similarly, my friends Eric Wright, Kildare Dobbs, Jack McLeod and Sheldon Zitner kept in touch and dragged me out for lunches, dinners and even radio interviews.

There was a great comfort in being at home again. The neighbours came calling. It was good to walk down Bloor Street again and drop into Book City and Dooney's, my local café. Here the regulars welcomed me back and watched over my comings and goings with an interest I wouldn't have expected. Recently, Jacob and I took a week off at the end of July. On my return, I discovered a concerned message from Graziano Marchese, the proprietor of Dooney's, on my answering machine. "Where are you? Are you still among the living? Please get in touch, because my friends would like to know." When I dropped in, somewhat alarmed that my seven-day holiday should so worry the Dooney's management and regulars, I found Graziano unable to contain his joy at seeing me alive and drinking my morning hot chocolate. I was plied with free raisin cookies, a fruit salad, orange juice. It was only when one of the regulars bedecked my fruit with whipped cream from behind the serving bar that Graz began to look like his old self and made jokes about how long it took me to read a short article in the paper about a property he had bought on Bloor Street. To a customer eyeing the section of the paper I was reading, Graz suggested, "Go out and get your own paper. Engel will take a week to finish the page he's reading."

While I was relearning the things I used to do and making myself useful around the house, I was still incubating the possibility of writing a new book. Apart from sitting in the window at Dooney's and washing up after dinner at home, there wasn't much to occupy my attention. I still bought books at Book City. I couldn't stop that; I was a browser by nature and could not walk past the bookstore without going in. I was still hard-wired for reading, in spite of my brain injury. Reading had been my bread and butter for too long to allow a mere stroke to trip me up. I went on browsing and buying. Only now I seemed to be bringing home cookbooks from every region on earth. I kept this up for some time, until I was trying to fit duplicate books into a shelf I had set aside for cookery tomes. Of course, this coincided with my return to the kitchen. By now I was preparing meals more often than earlier, although we went out to eat in the neighbourhood more often than not.

Bloor Street is well served by restaurants. One can choose to eat Thai, Japanese, Italian, Indian or Hungarian and crawl thither on hands and knees if necessary, they are so close to the house. We became regulars in a number of these establishments, got to know the chefs and wait staffs. We also ventured farther afield, looking for the novelty of a Peking duck, or dim sum at Kowloon on Baldwin Street on Sunday mornings. Jacob and I did this together or *en famille*, depending on how many of my older children or my in-laws were available.

Although this new spendthrift gourmandizing later brought a frown to the forehead of my taxman, it proved to be a rite of passage only. It was a transition from being in hospital to being at home. One reason I didn't cook more was because I got confused in the kitchen more than in any other part of the house.

We had occasional invitations to dinner, and some friends like Rosemary Kelly and Ann Barnett, Jonathan Friedman and Rona Abramowitz and my in-laws did more than their share. I don't think that the general falling off of invitations had anything to do with my new circumstances. I believe that most people are used to entertaining couples. For the most part, Jacob and I did not qualify as a couple. I won't go into more detail about this because I will probably get muddled.

I'm aware that my grasp of continuity is not of the first order. I'm sorry for this, but, dear reader, as the novelists used to say, not only am I trying to tell a story but, more importantly, I'm trying to also draw a picture of the state of my mind while I'm doing it. It is no longer a limpid pool, an unblemished crystal; it's what remains, it's what I've got to work with.

Over the past few years, because of the help I have been getting and probably because I refuse to accept my status as a *former* reader, my ability to read is steadily, if slowly, improving. At one point I noted that it was easier to find my place on a page after I had lost it. Earlier, I had to begin the page again at the top. My place once lost, stayed lost. Slowly, the fog that used to blur the print on a page had been lifting. Once-familiar words no longer looked like complete strangers but still needed to be "sounded out" the way I did in Grade One.

And still, I pondered the possibility of going on with my writing. Marla Roth had facilitated my note to Dr. Sacks. Was that going to be the end of it: a mention in a *New Yorker* article by someone else? Would it be so hard to breathe life back into my old private eye? Could I give it a chance?

10

AFTER ABOUT A HUNDRED DAYS away from home, the house looked strange and familiar at the same time. I was a visitor, a tourist in my own living room. It was as though a movie set had been assembled from sketches of the real house and its rooms. Most peculiar was my office. I looked at my computer with a strange feeling. My whole office, where I had written several of my books, resembled a diorama in a museum. Where was the velvet rope? Where the printed cards giving details and dates?

In a similar way, the owner of my desk and computer had become strange. Who had sat in this chair? Whose files and notebooks are these? Who is the owner of the simple treasures in these drawers? Who had jotted a note on this dusty block of paper? On scribbled stick-on notes, my own handwriting looked strange, unfamiliar.

I turned on the computer. The opening screens looked only vaguely familiar. Of course, I could not read any of the directions. Each successive screen was foreign and frightening. I turned the machine off. There would be a time to return to it, when I was feeling more like my old self.

I should say that this timorous approach to the computer was not being observed. Nor were subsequent experiments. I had no one at my back demanding that I return to work. If I had had an advance on a future book, my publisher did not remind me that I had done no work earning it. My family, my agent (Beverley Slopen) never pushed me. If I owed advanced money, I never heard about it. My eternal thanks and appreciation to whomever they may have been is hereby acknowledged.

After a few more visits home, circling around the computer, I turned it on again. This time, my son Jacob reminded me of its functions. After trying out such familiar formulas as "Now is the time for all good men to come to the aid of the party," I found that the strange monster was not biting my fingers, or bouncing into overdrive, or flashing strange warnings at me.

Spell-check warned me when I had misspelled a common word or used an improper vulgar one. (The machine is so much more prim and proper than I am.) Oddly, if I inserted an "8" or "0" in the middle of a word, the computer let it pass without comment. Why had it taken a stroke to make me notice such a thing? In general the computer and I got along well. My only problem occurred when my misspellings were inventive enough to hit upon an existing word; then the machine refused to tip me off.

Gradually, I made friends with the monster and it submitted to my reasonable wishes. Once these simple skills had been re-established, the time came for me to contemplate what I intended to write. I had nothing in mind. I had not written anything since I had completed my half of a novella that I wrote with Eric Wright. I'd finished my part only days before the stroke claimed me.

When I say I had written nothing since finishing *My Brother's Keeper*, I should mention that I have always kept a journal or notebook. My notebook was my memory book before I was handed a memory book at the Rehab. At its simplest, the book reminded me of appointments and birthdays. At its richest, it described my feelings about the events I sketched therein. The oldest of these diaries goes back to high-school days and recorded mostly comings and goings, rather than the emotional ups and downs of my younger self. I often described how I got to an event and left the event out completely.

While I was still in the hospital, I had written a note to myself in my diary about the day I was admitted.

Home again more than a hundred days later, I read the note again: "Major Health Episode." The language of that phrase leads me to believe I had been in the hospital or the Rehab some time before I wrote it; it reeks of medical jargon. The notes for the most part record visits from family and friends, the hospital routines and some descriptions of my fellow patients. Occasionally, I inserted a blood pressure reading or a question mark where a name escaped my moth-eaten memory. These notes, full of misspellings of simple words, do keep track of events with some humour as well as accuracy. Some of them are in another hand; perhaps my friend Laura's. But my own rather erratic handwriting is not absent for long. The writing instruments change many times as I turn the pages: various colours of inks and pencil. The size of my writing changes from page to page, from entry to entry, as though I was trying to rediscover my former conventional style. The letters slanted to the right in one entry, to the left in the next. I've seen the results of tests with insects under the influence of noxious fumes. My post-stroke handwriting was like a drunken beetle track.

When I thought about writing again—writing in a serious way, not simply in my journal or notes to myself, letters to friends and endless lists—at first I couldn't imagine where to start. I needed a subject. I hadn't been out in the world, I knew no inside story underneath the political horizon, I

July
Mon 30 ✓   2001

Tues 31 th Episode
Major Health
~~Eric~~ J + I + ~~art~~ Mt Sinai emergency —   Cottage trip cancelled because the weather
Eric's cottage non-viable for J + me
I was admitted   because of bad weather reports.
S'ade at home + had a strock instead.
- return from Eric's cottage. ← projected not
                                        actual.
- ~~~~

August
Wed   1   whose
                          ←   writing?
    - Skin of A Lion - Noreen
    - English short stories - Mary Conacher
    - Schubert, Maria Callas, Handel,
      Ellen F, Invisible Man + Brave World /-
      Gail Nobel

Thurs 2
    Cher + Jacob visited + we talked.
    - Jack? Kildare visited. Tests to see how much brean is left. I can write
    but have difficulty reading. I won't be able to make this
    out in half an hour. Somehow I'm not panicing.

was separated from big-city gossip and small-town intrigue. I had been out of the world for months. I could no longer keep things straight in my head. What business did I have imagining that I might go back to my old desk and begin again? I was clearly unfit for fiction. I turned off the computer and took a long walk.

The streets were crowded with people whose eyes didn't meet mine. I was so full of my own recent experiences I found it hard to imagine the lives of others. Then, of course, it hit me. My mother's old advice: *Write about what you know.* I'm sure all mothers of writers have repeated that old saw. And why not? It works. Even writers of speculative fiction often have to go back to their own pasts to find their material.

What I knew about now was my illness. I knew the hospital routines and the people around me. I could do a book that described what it was like to be out of things, flat on my back for a time with nurses and doctors ordering and reordering my days.

I remembered Josephine Tey's wonderful mystery novel *A Daughter of Time.* Tey's detective-hero is recovering in hospital from a serious accident in the line of duty and bored out of his mind while recuperating. He becomes fascinated by a picture of the infamous English king and child murderer, Richard III. The policeman sets out, metaphorically speaking, to find out the truth about history's most notorious uncle. It's a wonderful book, and I cannot recommend it highly enough.

Taking an acknowledged cue from Tey, I could have my hero, Benny Cooperman, work on a case while recovering in a hospital bed. Of course, detectives in books don't have strokes, so I decided that Benny would be suffering from a blow to his head. And since blows to the head that send a detective to hospital must come from mysterious circumstances, I had the rough beginnings of a plot. It was a good, workable idea. I was eager to get started.

Although my chief purpose was to write a ramping, stamping, thumping good story, I had the secondary scheme of including as much of the medical and hospital background as I could remember. At the same time—and this was important to me—I wanted to show what the world looked like through my eyes, the world as filtered through a battered brain. In a small way, I was trying to do for stroke victims what Dr. Temple Grandin did for autism.

I turned on the machine again. The succeeding screens looked slightly familiar, like high-school friends encountered at a twenty-fifth anniversary reunion. When an unfamiliar screen appeared, I yelled for help, and Jacob sprang to my side to explain and instruct once again. He was very good at putting a frazzled me back together again.

I began to work. My fingers remembered where the right keys were. I wrote a silly note to myself. I wrote another. I began to feel at home. Then, with a coffee to the right of me and a note about how to find "Help" on the menu to my left, I once more started in on a new document:

CHAPTER ONE

All well and good for a start. But could I complete a full English sentence? Could I manage a paragraph? Was a full page beyond my grasp? The question lurking behind this was, could I maintain a running thread through several sentences? Was the bouncing ball of thought more than my skills could sustain? Should I switch from writing novels to constructing haiku?

As I worked on, winkling out on the screen what I could no longer read back to myself a minute or two after I had written it, I began to wonder why I was going to so much trouble. What was driving me into this insane exercise? What was I trying to prove? I had written a dozen books; what more did I need to do? There was no need for me ever to put fingers to keyboard again.

But I couldn't get far with that argument. Writing was *what I did.* I was addicted to words. While I make no claims of being a serious artist, and I haven't been accused of creating literature yet, I needed to find out whether I could still commit crime fiction and get away with it. It was as close to a job as I had.

Slowly, I began to make friends with my disability. I found that I could still make out words on the screen. I made the words boldface; that helped. I made the letters bigger, moving from 12 point to 16. I tried to get rid of distractions, for I could no longer work with the radio on in the background. I forced the computer to help me out. It alerted me when my spelling went sour or I repeated words. Paragraph indentations reminded me of where I was working, and if I got hopelessly lost, I could find my place again with "Find," searching out key words I could never locate by simply reading. This worked as long as I could recall a word or a fragment of a sentence. It also saved my life when the numbering of the pages on the screen no longer matched the hard copy. Also, there was a difference between seeing a block of text and seeing words. The actual reading was so difficult that I started comparing different versions of the same text by their *shape*, not their content. Alternatively, when I was comparing the text on my screen to an earlier printed version, I was able to compare the words at the left-hand margins until they stopped matching. When they didn't match, something had been changed in one of the versions.

I tried a new program that read back to me the text I had just written. When the machine announced, in the voice of Stephen Hawking, "Massachusetts and Pennsylvania" although I had typed "Ma and Pa," I reluctantly discarded the program. Other mechanical aides failed me as well. They either gave me answers to questions I hadn't asked or they failed to understand what I needed.

The *given* in what I now started to write were the hundreds of details of hospital life. I drew from my time both in Mount Sinai and in the Rehab. I adapted the people I knew into fictional characters. I tried to recreate my own awakening consciousness as I was acquainted with its changes from day to day. I tried to recreate the lapses of memory as they affected me back then, and still to a lesser degree afflict me today. I began meditating on the underbelly of the plot that would bring about these changes in Benny Cooperman and also serve to form an acceptable story line.

The plot, as in many of my books, evolved during the writing of the book. Some strands of it were placed consciously with the hand of a writer who had had to construct solid plots before. But other touches got into the text without the author's conscious knowledge. For instance, the main device that revealed the name of the guilty party to the detective was fully in place before the author was aware that he had done it. Perhaps part of this is the result of my illness, but I suspect that it is simply part of the always mysterious creative process.

Without being aware of it, I had started kidnapping characters into my head as they walked down the hall and talked to me over lunch. I was guileless in the process; I thought I was simply observing what was going on around me. Unfortunately, I have never had a great memory for overheard dialogue, so most of the material within quotation marks is reconstituted from dry notes, not purloined from the Rehab. But the feeling and other details are right on.

While I was becoming more and more excited about getting involved with creating characters and situations, I was also excited about the fact that I was actually beginning to do it. To write again. I could still find the words, the phrases and situations in my head. I could remember what I'd done during my last session simply by reading the last sentence I'd completed. That's the way it has always been with me: I can never remember what happened when I broke off writing until I read the last line again. Then it all comes back to me.

Oh, there were times when words failed me, when I scratched my head and ransacked the alphabet to surrender up the word on the tip of my tongue. Sometimes it happened; more often I had to wait until I was thinking of something else. Ideas came to me and vanished before I could get them down. A brief interruption might evaporate a scheme still developing in my head. Yes, there were frustrations. Sometimes I thought I was on the rim of madness, but the good feeling of being back at work again carried me through the rough patches. I felt like shouting "Richard is himself again!"

11

WHEN I WAS FINALLY CLEAR OF THE REHAB, Laura, Jacob and I made our way down to New York City in my Volvo with Laura at the wheel. (One of the fastest things in Canadian medicine is the speed at which the hospital reports strokes to the Motor Vehicles Branch of the Department of Highways. These amiable people quickly snap up drivers' licenses with a stroke of their own.) Oliver Sacks had invited me to drop in whenever I found myself in Manhattan, and I communicated to him that we were planning just such a visit. It was a little before St. Patrick's Day, 2002.

The purpose of the trip, of course, was to finally meet Dr. Sacks. But why? I wasn't a collector of celebrities. I didn't think he was a magician. I didn't expect that he might have a miraculous cure for my poor brain. I think I wanted to communicate with a fellow writer about the way my alexia looked from where I was standing. I was reminded of the movie *Cat Ballou*, with Jane Fonda and Lee Marvin. In it, Marvin, as a drunken, gone-to-seed gunfighter, is informed by an old-timer, "Your eyes look terrible!" To this the gunfighter replies, "You should see them from *this* side." I guess what I wanted to see Oliver Sacks about was to tell him what my brain looked like from *this* side.

The weather on the road was perfect, so perfect I almost forgot the frustration of not being able to sit behind the steering wheel myself. It's funny about the driving. I thought that being in the driver's seat was tied up with who I was, that macho thing. But it wasn't, and I was surprised that I could let forty years of driving in North America, Europe and Asia vanish so quietly into my past without a whimper or stab of lingering pain.

Jacob had never travelled in the United States before, although he had been to England and Ireland. Laura, because of her frequent meetings with business colleagues, was an old New York hand. As I mentioned earlier, when younger, I had scalped tickets to *My Fair Lady* on 54th Street and, more recently, I had for a half-dozen years attended the annual meeting of the Mystery Writers of America. So there would be good friends to see as well as the museums and galleries.

We broke the journey through upper New York State, staying at a recommended hotel and eating well. For all of us it was a happy trip, full of expectations. We slipped into the Big Apple through a side door from New Jersey. The hotel, nestled in the bowels of downtown Manhattan, placed us within a short distance of Dr. Sacks's office. The next morning, Jacob decided to stay in bed while Laura and I alone made the short journey to the doctor's office.

Dr. Sacks worked in an old part of Greenwich Village. After a short wait, Laura and I were admitted to his consulting room. On a cabinet lay a stack of the doctor's new book: *Uncle Tungsten: Memories of a Chemical Boyhood.* On one wall hung a large framed copy of the periodic table of elements, each element given its atomic number and weight, all arranged in order. Of course then, without having read his new book, I was unable to guess the chart's significance in Sacks's life. On the wall behind where I was sitting I noticed that my name appeared on a chalkboard. Should the doctor have momentarily forgotten my name, it was there where he could read it without embarrassment. What a sensible approach to a universal problem. After seeing that, I felt sure I was going to get along with him.

When the doctor appeared, he looked familiar to me. Of course—it was the manner and look that the actor Robin Williams had so successfully captured in the film *Awakenings.*

Although there was a large desk handy, Dr. Sacks sat facing us in a chair like the ones we occupied. Laura sat to my left, I think. The doctor asked us a barrage of questions. I noticed he listened to our answers with care before replying. There was a distinct pause between answers and new questions. One could sense the mental activity going on as he reflected on each of our answers. He was thoughtful, but by no means solemn. He was easy to talk to, a prerequisite for all medical practitioners. I think he gave us coffee, but I'm not certain. The visit was one of those moments that, even at the time, you know you'll want to remember forever. Unfortunately, the desire to remember isn't itself the stuff of memory. I can remember a face that looked like a version of Robin Williams, his reflective pauses after Laura or I had spoken. Despite the cordiality, there was no mistaking the serious underpinnings of our chat. We were both working hard. Later, when I was reading the first part of his autobiography, I was reminded of the description of his father manfully trying to play the piano with thick, unvirtuosic fingers.

In a generous and friendly gesture, he presented me with a copy of *Uncle Tungsten*, which I got him to sign. At the same time, I gave him a copy of my most recent Cooperman. Later, while reading about the author's childhood, I often saw in my mind the table of the elements as it hung on his wall. To me it seemed to be a centre around which a shy youngster organized the elements of his life.

While he was signing the book and making a personal inscription, I summoned up enough courage to ask him if he would write an introduction to the novel I was then working on. As I said the words, I felt I was asking one favour too many. With his characteristic pause before speaking, he told me to send him the book when it was finished. This put the ball back in my court; it was a challenge to finish the manuscript. It was the carrot that I needed to get on with the job of completing the work.

Back in Toronto, I resumed work on my book with a will. It seemed to be going faster now. I could still dish it out at my old speed, but got into trouble when I had to go back and read what I'd just done. But at the back door of my mind I ruminated on the New York visit, recalling the details of Dr. Sacks's office, his manner and kindness. I'm not sure why I've done this. More important, I'm not certain why I went to see him in the first place. I didn't expect to become a patient; he didn't recommend a specialist who was able to get me reading again. Perhaps I felt as though I'd taken my complaint to the chairman of the board. I didn't feel as isolated. I knew now that there were others who were similarly cut down.

12

EVERY DAY I WORKED ON MY MANUSCRIPT. I found some of my characters almost ready-made in my memory. Others needed to be invented. A plot needed to be manufactured. I found that my mind was still quick enough to invent things. I recognized the familiar signs of creative harmony and chaos, loss of nerve and stasis. Here, even the signs that told me that the work was not going well supported me because they were familiar landmarks of the snags of creativity. I had been there before, so I didn't panic.

It was easy to invent strategies like this. The hardest thing to do was to remember whether an idea had already been expressed in the text. By looking for a key word in the "Find" feature, I could put an end to my anxiety about unwanted repetition. I noticed that most of my spelling mistakes were with the initial letter. Often the wrong letter was the first letter of the following word. My wounded brain was still moving faster than my fingers. In order to keep a section of the manuscript freshly in mind, I often tracked a key word and made note of what page it appeared on and in what context. It was almost as good as reading.

My chief help and support came from friends like Griffiths Cunningham, an old friend who also comes from St. Catharines, Nancy Vichert, a dear friend going back to high-school days and Donald Summerhayes, who preceded me at McMaster by a year or so. They read my text to me while I made notes about the tone and structure of the work as I heard it read at a normal pace. Although the work must have been an infinite bore to them, it was a great help to me. By this time I was able to make notes to myself that I could read back afterwards. My main failing, apart from spongy passages and longueurs of boring repetition, was that I would forget where I had intended to go some few paragraphs back. When the text was read back to me, it seemed to twist, like the monkey's paw in my hand, as the sense changed from what I had intended to say to what I actually ended up saying. As Grif or Don read back to me, I could adjust my wandering trajectory and readdress my sentences to the right destination.

13

AS THE WEEKS AND MONTHS FOLLOWED one another, like a time-passing device in the movies—pages falling from the calendar or blossoms, leaves and fruit following each other in a movie from the 1940s—I worked at my disabilities on several fronts. I regularly met with friends. While this was always enjoyable, it was also useful in reminding me who I used to be. Meeting with friends at literary events served the same purpose, once I learned not to wince when I couldn't remember a name when greeted warmly by a friend.

In the old days, before my stroke, I used to leap into a conversation whenever I had an idea to contribute. Now I sometimes forget the point I am about to make before an opening occurs in the flow of talk. So, I have become shy about jumping into the cut and thrust, because my contribution may have evaporated by the time every eye is turned in my direction. To try to snag my thoughts and hold on to them while talk was going on around me, I developed strategies to keep things straight in my head. Names were the hardest to remember. They were always on the tip of my tongue, holding up the flow of conversation. I developed elaborate techniques for remembering some names, as I had with my Rehab nurse Kathy Nelson. In trying the other day to recall the name Norman, I went back to the mystery writer Ross Macdonald, whose real name was Kenneth Millar. That gave me my first clue. Miller, this time "er" and not "ar," is the family name of the Ontario legislator Norman Miller, whose hospitality I enjoyed for many years before his entry into politics. I used Norman, or someone like him, in a story once. But, more importantly for my memory, thinking of him gave me the name Norman, which is what I was looking for in the first place. Other memory tricks are just as complicated, and just as personal and quirky.

My long-suffering agent, Beverley Slopen, suggested that I needed someone to help me deal with the piled-up paperwork on the kitchen table: bills, invitations, notices, letters both professional and personal. That someone turned out to be Madeline Grant, a trained librarian, who was a whiz with paper. I had a hard time remembering her name, although we were good friends and saw one another almost weekly. When I was at sea trying to remember her name, I tried to recall the name of the owner of a summer camp where I once worked as a counsellor. The name was Granovsky, which they later changed to Grant. It seems an elaborate route to follow, but when simply running through the alphabet doesn't work, I'm forced to use this method. And the above example is a fairly simple and straight-forward one.

Long after the acute need for Madeleine to sort me out had passed, we continued to meet because of the fun of it. We talked about Bloomsbury and the expatriate writers in Paris during the 1920s and ended up having a lunch at Dooney's down the street.

~

I WORKED AT MY MEMORY, but there wasn't much of it left. After a newscast, I could not call to mind what the top three items were. So it was then, and so it remains. My memory is shot for good. It's a major disability, but the body becomes aware of it only in the act of trying to remember particular items. It works like an old sports injury: you only notice it when you try to get back into the game. In this way, the disability is hidden from the sufferer. When I'm not trying to pitch a curve ball, I forget that I can't do it any more. In that way it's not like an amputation, which is there whether one is trying to walk or not.

~

SOMEWHERE, A MONTH OR TWO AFTER I got out of the Rehab, Alice, one of the two family cats, died, leaving her brother, Henry, to survive her. Jacob was wounded by this family shock. Alice was the first change in the family since Janet died in June 1998. I know that to some, the comparison is invidious. What outsiders might consider a trivial event can have serious consequences. My being felled by a mentally challenging condition didn't make things any easier. We buried Alice in the garden, where Henry joined her a year later.

~

I BELIEVE THAT A HOUSE REFLECTS the character of its owner. Some houses are showplaces, some are—what's the cliché?—"tools for living." My house is no different. It used to look like the home of a pair of freelance writers: books and papers all over the place, a dining room turned into a library, an upstairs bedroom converted into an office. As Jacob grew, his bedroom changed along with him. When

Janet died, her influence and sense of style slowly faded in some places and was preserved in others. We were never the tidiest of householders; messy, but tolerably clean, I guess. Looking around the house now, after I've been out of the hospital for a few years, I can see the new me reflected in what I see. The house is still clean. The pictures on the walls have been rearranged, and there are more of them. And some treasures that had been hidden away are now on display. But the bookshelves are still in a state of confusion. They say that a woman's purse and a man's workbench are places where character may be read. I hope no one reads my character from the confusion of my book shelves.

The house has become an untended library with books all over the place. There is no sense or order in the piles and rows of tomes on the floor. One would have thought that with my limited powers I would have stopped collecting books, but I haven't. I'm worse now than I have ever been.

One day after I came out of hospital, I found that my mind was easily confused by accumulated newspapers. I disliked seeing them piled up and unread, and when they were opened and spread out they made for further confusion. I'd lose things under them. I'd have to clear away the papers looking for a pen or cheque book or stamp. Sometimes it led to a near frenzy of disorder and my mind became nearly deranged by the confusion. This situation was solved by stopping delivery of the papers. Now I get my information electronically. But while that solves part of the problem, I am surprised at myself: I continue to buy books. I was always a good customer of my friend Frans Donker's Book City. I used to be in and out of there several times a week. What surprises me is that I remain a good customer and that I continue to buy books.

Books have always been my vice. Happily, in our society, it need not be a secret vice, although I have been in many fine homes without a book showing. But now, when I perhaps might have cleared away all of the library to make way for electronic information-processing machines, I keep on bringing books home like stray cats. I can't stop.

Perhaps it's a refusal to accept my acquired limitations. Maybe I'm pretending that all is well with me. I don't think so. As I said earlier, I'm hard-wired to literacy. Why else would *A Pilgrim's Progress* be lying on the kitchen table as I write this? Why else are copies of *A Moveable Feast, The Hittites, The Norman Conquest* and *Down the Yellow Brick Road: The Making of The Wizard of Oz* piled next to my bed? Why, at my age, am I reading Dryden, and Byron? If I can find out the answer to that, I will have solved the biggest puzzle of my life.

14

WHEN I HAD DONE AS MUCH AS I COULD to get Benny Cooperman in and out of trouble in *Memory Book,* by myself, I asked my editors at Penguin to help me with the final editing. Through them I was able to work with two of the best editors in the country, Mary Adachi and Cynthia Good. Mary had been my copy editor on half a dozen books in the past, so we knew one another and I looked forward to her tea and snacks. Cynthia at that time was moving from the top job at Penguin to a freelance association that would leave her time to engage in more independent professional activities. She and I had worked together many times on the final editing of a manuscript. I looked forward to working with both of these tireless professionals once again.

Because I could no longer read as quickly nor as accurately as I had in the past, I was expecting that the manuscript would need months of work. In fact we managed it in not much more time than it used to take. Having read the manuscript, the editors, one after the other, went through the text marking problem areas with bright little Post-it notes, which I dealt with back in my office one at a time. When there were more serious problems, we discussed them face to face while I made notes. If I could not read the notes that were left sticking to the pages, I went back for a typewritten translation. This worked out well for all concerned. At the same time, I began to notice that my ability to read notes in other people's handwriting was slowly improving.

The book, even in its earliest stages, was pretty sound. There were unnecessary repetitions and contradictions, of course. There always were at this stage. There were new problems as well, things that hadn't happened before. Rereading the text, it was now clear to the author and his editors that I often began a narrative with its direction and conclusion in mind, but by the time I got to the end of a passage, I had forgotten where it was headed and veered off on a tangent. I would complete the section with a new idea or thought. Together, we reworked most of the problems. In other cases, the twisted ideas were left intact to illustrate the sort of mental problems that Benny was experiencing.

It was crucial to me that the book should show Benny's mental condition. That was more important than forgetting a major plot point or leaving a key character dangling in limbo at the end.

When I had finished my first draft of the manuscript, I wrote Dr. Sacks to tell him of my progress:

I have finished my book . . . As an author, you'll know how meaningless that word *finish* is. What I mean to say is that I have reached the ending for the first time. How many more times will I have to finish it before it leaves the house for the last time? From now on it will be a matter of rewriting and reworking the material . . . My publisher has lent me an editor, who has marked certain parts of the manuscript for my attention . . . I am able to deal with the simple problems of spelling, syntax and repetition by taking them one at a time, orienting myself on the page by making use of paragraph breaks to show me where I am . . . It remains hard to get a fix of the flow of a book working this way. I can replace divots and monkey about to my heart's content, but I wonder whether I will be able to see serious plot or design flaws in time.

Today (some time in late May 2004) I got a long letter from Oliver Sacks, in which he offered to write a short introduction to Memory Book, the MS of which I sent him a few weeks ago.

It's a good long letter, in which he spotted a few of the spots I hoped he'd find. Although he says he's only read ½ of the MS, he has well read what he's read.

Thurs, 30 Sept. 7:30 - 9:30
Meet Eric @ 5:30 @ recept. Int. Fest. of authors ; Lakeside Terrace, 235 Queen W then go to Ave Rd. Art School for the above.

Lupino Loy = singer of The Lambeth Walk

Get converter cable for tape recorder + tapes cassettes. + batteries

One of the things I learned to look forward to as a writer was the thrill of sending a manuscript out of the house on its way to the publisher. It's a wonderful feeling, like sending a child off to school for the first time. It's the beginning of a book's journey out into the world to make its own way through the battlefields of the marketplace, through the minefields of reviews, the hazards of marketing and the whim of the buyer.

Of course, I was quite wrong. As I said to Dr. Sacks, a book leaves the author's study many times and comes back many times; there is always last-minute tinkering to be done. The various messenger services grow rich on these last-minute changes. Each time you send a manuscript out the door, you hope it's for the last time. You want the next appearance of the book to be in galleys or proofs or, even, in its final form. Not damned likely! The last-minute fine-editing slows down the process and leads to the belief that the manuscript is attached to the upstairs office in my house by a ghostly elastic that snaps back whenever the book arrives on a new desk at the publisher's.

Then, one day, when you are at work on another project, a package arrives from the publisher. You open it. Inside: cover art! For the first time you see the image of what the book will come to be. An icon, new-born. You read the copy, examine the artwork. You hear an inner voice say: "Yes, this is good. I can live with this."

I still have the first glimpse I saw of the book jacket stuck on my refrigerator door. It shows a hospital building at night from the outside. All is dark on the street. The only brightness comes from a single light illuminating one of the hospital rooms: a very unusual sight to see in a busy downtown hospital at any time at night. The atmosphere is vaguely mysterious, and suspense clings to the shadowed walls and grounds scarcely brightened by a shaded full moon coldly looking down on the scene.

The hospital on the book jacket is not the hospital described in the novel. Benny's room was not on the top floor of the building. But the atmosphere is right: dark, brooding clouds and trees with shadowed foliage. A celebrated English writer of crime fiction once told me that in one of her novels a particular van is featured. The brand and model are mentioned on several occasions as it drives menacingly through the darkened streets of London. Yet, on the book jacket, another van is depicted. When she protested to the publisher, she discovered exactly how powerless a writer is once the writing is done.

I was told that my book cover was a "selling cover" even if it departed from the reality of the scene. My informant must have been right, because the book has done very well in the world. Its sales have been better than most of my other books. So perhaps my picky criticism of the cover should send me back to write more books for others to print and design covers for.

Soon there are page proofs to examine. The editor asks me to mark corrections in one colour and expansions or changes in another. I enlist the help of friends to help me in this, for me, very drawn-out task. It was as difficult for me to recognize a word spelled incorrectly as it was for me to ride bareback across the Pampas on a goat. But with the help of Grif Cunningham and Don Summerhayes, the job was done at last.

Then, the long-awaited afterword by Dr. Sacks. It took me a few days to get up enough courage to read it. I don't know what I was expecting. I knew he wouldn't savage the book, but I was still uneasy. Once again I felt like a patient in hospital, stripped, covered only by my scant cotton gown and examined by a cohort of specialists and their attending nurses and interns. Gradually, I summoned the needed courage and began to read the eleven pages. The reading, of course, took forever. Eleven pages was still an Everest of a read, a marathon of sounding out the syllables, nose to the paper, and moving snail-like down the pages. But that was only part of my trouble. I knew that with perseverance I would get to the end. My problem was more subtle. I was about to read words that might change my life. What if he said that progress in battling alexia was useless? What if he held out no hope for me? Was I doomed forever to sound out my words like a beginning reader?

Moments after I started reading the afterword, I could hear in my head that calm, reasoned voice I had heard first in his Greenwich Village consulting room all those months before. This was the voice of an informed *friend*. I read on:

> There have been a number of recent books that have incorporated medical or neurological themes (detectives with Tourette's syndrome, detectives with autism, etc.)—and indeed this goes back, in suspense novels, to the fiction of Wilkie Collins in the nineteenth century. But *Memory Book* has a unique depth and authenticity, because Howard Engel has known and traversed all that he writes about. He has, as Bertrand Russell would say, "knowledge by experience," and no knowledge by description can match this.

What Dr. Sacks said was what I'd hoped to hear. I heard my inner voice saying, "I knew that." And then I came upon forgotten information, which I had to admit had slipped from my non-adhesive memory. It was very flattering and complimentary, which I didn't mind at all. Not that I was starved for compliments, or that my ego had been bruised by my experiences on University Avenue. It was more that I had to recognize that I *had* done a remarkable thing, and, now that it was over, I needed to know, like everybody else, how I had done it. To a great degree the piece that Dr. Sacks added to my book helped me as well as my readers to understand what I had managed to do.

When I had read it, I dashed off a note of thanks and sent it to Dr. Sacks in Manhattan. A call from him told me that he wanted to incorporate some of the new information in my note into his afterword. He sent me a second draft, which was even better. This is the one that was printed in the book.

Since that time Oliver Sacks and I have kept in touch with one another. He calls me when he visits Toronto, and we had breakfast together at his hotel in November 2005, when he was here to address a medical group of some kind. When he inquired about my battle with reading, I tried to describe the sensation of not being able to bring a page of print into focus without expending a major effort of visual concentration. I described it as giving the page a "double whammy" and began to explain the origin of that phrase: it comes from the old comic strip *L'il Abner.* Dr. Sacks interrupted my explanation. "Al Capp was my cousin," he said.

Some writers keep a close watch on sales. I am not one of them. If I have a gift of some sort, it has nothing to do with business skills. There are writers I know, and I've heard them praised for it, that haunt the publisher's office, telephone their editors after midnight and generally make editors, publishers and publicists wish they had chosen another line of work. Nor do I phone my agent with clever suggestions for interviews or angles for feature stories. I don't do this, not because I think they don't do any good, but simply because I'm not very good at it. I do have a file of clippings, of course. While I'm not an egomaniacal egotist, I'm not dead either. I stay away from the publisher's office. I do not wear out my eyes reading the fine print in *Publishers Weekly* or the *Kirkus Reviews.* I know that I have no insights into the business of publishing, so I stay away from it until my advice is requested. When I begin to get antsy and curious, it's high time I started thinking of writing another book. It's the old separation of Church and State. I respect both, but I stay as far away from the business side of writing as I can. I feel like that character in *Three Men on a Horse:* once they force the man who always knows which horse is going to finish in the money to put down a bet himself, the fun of it goes; his gift evaporates. And maybe, at bottom, I'm afraid that if I read too many pieces about what a good writer I am, I'll begin to believe it. That way madness lies. Once I begin to think of myself as special, that's the end. That's why I can never remember which paper had a favourable review in it, or which paper or magazine has sent a photographer around to see me. It's a matter of self-defence. Because once I begin believing in the press I've been getting over the years, I'm as good as finished. I should go back to scalping theatre tickets.

15

WHEN MEMORY BOOK WAS PUBLISHED, I already had a chapter or two sketched out for a sequel. In it, I decided to take Benny away from his comfortable perch in Grantham, Ontario, to a place far beyond his experience. I decided to take him to Asia. After the surprises in *Memory Book*, I had to find something new and unusual for him to discover and be initially bewildered by. That's why *East of Suez* is set where it is. I needed a dose of bravura for an encore. To get the setting right, I had all of those old Warner Brothers or Columbia black-and-white movies of the 1930s and '40s to draw upon for atmosphere. In fact, that was part of the original idea, to revisit again all those Saturday matinees of my youth, where Jack Holt, Lloyd Nolan or Lyle

Talbott looked beyond the bead curtains of shadowy orien-
tal nightclubs, where Peter Lorre or Turhan Bey manipu-
lated arms or drug deals while Maria Montez, Ida Lupino
or Jane Russell sang sultry torch songs. Somewhere in the
background lurked George Macready, with his scar, or the
pock-marked Joseph Calleia. I've probably got the actors
and studios mixed up, but my memory of those matinees
is part of the stew of my personal ancient past.

Apart from the movies, I had the help of my old McMaster friend, Professor Garry Thaler, who spent most of his
holidays enjoying the real modern equivalents of those
shadowy settings in Thailand. He showed me hundreds of
photographs and told me what I would have seen across
the street. These pictures, together with the long, descriptive letters he sent me, often included descriptions and stories he'd sent to other friends. Buttressed by old movies, I
felt comfortable enough to set Benny Cooperman loose in
this, to him and me, strange environment. Here, of course,
Benny didn't know the language, he couldn't read the street
signs even if he wanted to because of his alexia. He couldn't
even read the few signs written in English unless he stopped
and stared at them for five minutes.

Benny was no world traveller to begin with; to take him
out of Grantham and place him on his own on the shores
of the Andaman Sea was an idea that I have been carrying about with me for some time. Pushing Benny off his

comfortable perch has been fun to do from the very first book in the series, *The Suicide Murders*, in 1980, right up to the present moment.

As with the writing of all of my books, when the writing was easy, I seemed to be there simply to attend to the computer; the writing looked after itself. But when the work was not going well, I was most certainly involved. Earlier, I compared it to the unpleasant task of trying to roll a half-ton of raw liver uphill.

I am still getting in trouble because of my alexia. Just the other day I bought a jar of jam. Or so I thought it was. It turned out to be cranberry sauce and not jam at all. While I enjoy cranberry sauce, there is hardly anything easier to make. It was jam I wanted. The old alexia keeps bringing in its revenges.

And so it goes. There are good days and bad. At times I find the way hard and confusing, but I get my reward the following day when the way is easier to find. Hard work pays off. But both the difficult times and the easy times are all part of the same thing. The way up and the way down are one and the same, as T. S. Eliot is always pointing out. And, even on the days when my confusion is so great I want to junk the whole manuscript, I know I'm doing what I want to do, that my work and I suit one another. We deserve each other.

Epilogue

I AM WRITING THIS IN THE WINTER OF 2007. I have long ago said farewell to all of my therapists. I am not now taking any treatment at all for my stroke or for my memory loss. When I see old hospital and Rehab friends, it is because I have been asked to come and speak to them about my case and how I've been able to cope. Twice, with Michelle Cohen, I have talked on an inter-hospital television network set up so that we could address several groups of interested professionals in hospitals in and outside this city. In connection with writing this book, I have been in touch again with several of the people who appear in the foregoing pages. From time to time I still see my nurse Kathy Nelson, who made my stay at the Rehab memorable.

Writing these two books, the novel and the memoir, was different. In the case of the former, I had no idea whether I could bring it off. This one was written with the assurance of someone who has done it before. As I've mentioned, I also have a new book of fiction in the works. The writing of fiction is, for me at least, a much more relaxed function than writing about oneself. Autobiography may be the ultimate fiction, but it lacks the freedom of making it all up. Memoirs unleash a self-consciousness that squeezes the creative process into a straitjacket that cannot be easily shaken off. Still, as Huck Finn says, I tried to tell the truth in the main, though I may have stretched things from time to time.

~

I LEARNED TO LIVE WITH CONFUSION. I made a friend of it. In my day-to-day diary of those days, I often confused Sundays and Mondays. So, looking at the calendar now, I find that I forgot to go to meet my university friends on Mondays, because I had scheduled them on Sundays. Some invitations that came by mail never made it to the appointment book because, as I used to say as a child, "Just because." On the whole, I didn't miss much in those days and I don't miss much nowadays. Back then I arrived at Massey College a day late to meet Prince Philip, and last week I arrived two days late to a barbecue in the back yard of a good friend. So, in that sense, my life can be compared to someone carrying water in his hands: most of it is lost along the way, but a few drops arrive where they are needed.

My memory works in mysterious ways, mysterious to me at least. When I try to recall the name of a film actor, the street address of a friend, the title of a book, its author or any flat-footed fact, I can rarely apprehend it. I can remember peripheral things that support the answer that eludes me, but often it doesn't help. Yesterday I was trying to think of the actor Harrison Ford. I went through the alphabet in my mind several times without luck. (I still do this when I fail to be able to place a name with a familiar face. It mostly works.) I named a film or two in which he starred, and failed to name others that suddenly hid their titles from me. I did remember that his name cited two American presidents. I was able to lasso the name a moment later. This sort of thing happens every day, and every day I try to find the shortcut that will clear the mess in my head. I suppose that all of this stems from the original alexia sine agraphia, but I am uncertain whether elements of creeping old age aren't mixed in somewhere. Most of my friends can't remember names.

I must not distort my mental state; I'm only trying to describe it. I was almost whole. At a lunch table, with the usual Friday collection of academics and writers, I was able to contribute to the conversation as well as keep up with it. I think that there, in conversation, I was at my best. I could measure the improvements.

I mustn't try to let myself off the hook, either. I *was* in trouble, and I shouldn't whitewash it away. While looking at the fruit in a supermarket, I can remember wondering what *orange* was. Were the oranges more yellow than they should be? Were the tomatoes really red, or were they orange or yellow? It was as though my mind was challenging the produce to behave so as to coincide with my Platonic images of what they should be. I know that perceptions are always changing: coming from a shower into a warm room seems cool; we don't notice the dying light when we are outside the way we do when we are looking out a window into the darkening back yard.

~

MY READING IS STILL SLOW AND PONDEROUS. I get my news through talking to well-informed people at lunch and listening to the radio. I continue to write, but the problems that existed when I saw Dr. Sacks a few years ago persist. The techniques I developed for overcoming the difficulties still work for me. Perhaps I have become a more careful reader. An example of this care appeared the other day, when I found a misspelling in a note at the front of a well-known author's book thanking his careful editors and proofreaders. But I am still no speed-reader. I still have half a dozen books on the go sitting on available flat surfaces around the house. My son Jacob is now a towering teenager about to enter university. My older children have distinguished themselves in their fields and still keep in touch with their old man. My own life has been made sweeter recently by an alliance with Susan Milojevic, a charming, funny, intelligent woman who in addition to enriching the life of this codger has acted the part of midwife in the birth of this short book. I am, as Dickens said, "recalled to life."

Afterword
by Oliver Sacks, MD

SEVERAL YEARS AGO, I FOUND MYSELF THINKING about the problem of alexia, an inability to read resulting from damage to a particular area in the occipital cortex, the visual part of the brain. I had been seeing a patient, an eminent pianist, who had become unable to read music, and then to read words. She saw them as clearly as ever, but now they had become "unintelligible . . . meaningless . . . just marks on paper." All this my patient had explained to me in a letter, for she was perfectly able to write, though unable to read what she had written.

Shortly after this, I received a letter from the writer Howard Engel, who had also had a striking case of alexia.

Soon afterward we met, and he told me his story, which he has now—against all odds—written himself in *The Man Who Forgot How to Read.*

One morning a few months earlier, he said, he had got up as usual, dressed and made breakfast, and then went outside to get his newspaper. But *The Globe and Mail,* he found, seemed to have undergone an uncanny transformation, and had apparently been printed in "Serbo-Croatian" that morning. This immediately reminded him of an odd case history he had read a few years earlier, my own "Case of the Colorblind Painter." He remembered in particular how my patient, Mr. I., following a traffic accident, had found himself unable to read the police accident report—how he saw print of different sizes and types, but could make nothing of it, and said it looked like "Greek" or "Hebrew" to him. Engel wondered if he, like the painter, had developed alexia, and perhaps, without realizing it, had had a stroke.

He went to the local emergency room, where it was ascertained that he had indeed had a small stroke, affecting a limited area of the visual parts of the brain, the occipital cortex, on the left side. It became apparent that there were also some visual problems besides the alexia: a quarter of the visual field was missing, high up on the opposite side, and there were some difficulties in recognition of shapes and colours, though these were mild compared to the impossibility of recognizing words or individual letters or numbers by sight.

Alexia, or "word-blindness," as it was originally called, has been recognized by neurologists since the late nineteenth century, and has always been a source of fascination, for one thinks of reading and writing as going together, and it seems bizarre, counterintuitive, that someone should be able to write but be quite unable to read what they have just written. It has often been observed that this alexia sine agraphia is a purely visual problem; people with alexia have no difficulty, for instance, recognizing letters or words if they are traced on the hand. The intactness of such tactile reading, as well as of speech recognition, showed that Engel did not have aphasia—a disturbance of language in general—but a pure word blindness, the result of certain areas of the visual cortex being cut off, by the stroke, from the language areas on the same side of the brain. There was nothing wrong with his eyes, and he could *see* letters perfectly well, but he could not interpret them.

We normally think of reading as a seamless, indivisible act. One has to encounter a disconnection such as Engel now had to realize that reading, in fact, involves a number of separate processes and stages, from basic perceptual processes to higher-level abilities to decipher and interpret what one is seeing.

It was a huge relief for Engel to realize that, though he could not read, his ability to *write* was unimpaired—even though he might not be able to read what he had written. For while his other symptoms—the field defects, the problems with colours and shapes—gradually diminished over a few days, the alexia remained unchanged. As a prolific writer and an omnivorous reader, accustomed to reading newspapers every morning and a dozen or more books a week, he started to wonder what alexia would mean for him—and whether he would have to give up his life and work as a writer.

Being able to write without the ability to read what he had written might be all right for a short letter or memorandum, even a poem, an essay, a page or two—but how could he hope to go back to his previous work, to write a whole book, an elaborate story of crime and detection, to do all the corrections and revisions and redrafting a writer must do, without being able to read? He would have to get others to read for him, or perhaps get one of the new software programs that would allow him to scan what he had written and hear it read back to him by a computer. But either of these would still involve a radical shift, from the visuality of reading, the sight of words on a page, to an essentially auditory mode of perception and thought. Would this be possible?

After a week in hospital, Engel moved to a rehabilitation hospital, where he was to spend the next eight weeks or so, and here he began to study himself, what he could and could not do. With his therapists, he explored new—sometimes radically new—ways of trying to read and to spell (which he also discovered, at this point, was very difficult for him).

Engel's alexia affected not only his ability to read but his internal visual imagery as well. He could not "see" words *as* words in his mind's eye any more than he could perceive them as words when they were printed before him. Lacking this internal imagery, he had to employ other strategies for spelling and for deciphering words. The simplest of these, he found (since his writing remained unimpaired), was to write a word in the air with his finger.

Sometimes, if he looked at a word, a couple of letters would suddenly jump out at him and be recognized—for example, the *bi* in the middle of his editor's name, though the letters before and after this remained unintelligible. (Thus guessing or inference to complete a word using such scattered clues became extremely important.) Such "chunking" was, he thought, similar to the way that most of us begin learning to read as children, even though we later learn to perceive words as a whole. Normally the perception of letter clusters, syllables or words, as well as inferences and hypotheses based on such perceptions, become instantaneous and unconscious, so that we can read fluently and swiftly, and are able to attend consciously to the meaning (and perhaps the beauty) of written language. But it was very different for Engel at this point, since it was only occasionally that a recognizable fragment of a word might jump out, surrounded by an entire page of "Serbo-Croatian."

With help from his therapists, Engel learned to slowly and laboriously puzzle out the names of street signs or grocery aisles, or headlines in a newspaper. This, even in the absence of normal reading, made day-to-day life possible.

Engel's weeks in the rehabilitation hospital proved to be a revelation as to how the mind works and how seemingly automatic neurological processes can fall apart and have to be reconstructed in other ways. But it was a very rich human experience as well, and Engel, with his novelist's eye and ear fully intact, got to know his nurses and his fellow patients, their feelings about illness, their idiosyncrasies, and the intricacies of their lives. Being a patient, experiencing and observing the whole atmosphere of hospital life, stimulated his imagination, and it was at this point that the idea for a new book came to him, one in which his alter ego, Benny Cooperman, would be a patient in a hospital ward with alexia (as well as a few other neurological problems), and in which he would solve a mystery—the mystery of how he had ended up brain-damaged in a hospital ward—without ever leaving the ward.

Once he was home, Engel moved into high gear with his writing, and the manuscript of his new book rapidly took shape. Within a few weeks, he completed the first draft, and he wrote to me at this point.

I found [his] letter astonishing. How was Engel able to deal with the "simple" problems of spelling, syntax and repetition when (as he wrote in his letter) "the old casual recognition of familiar words remains occluded"? The answer, or a partial answer, he wrote, lay in decoding English print as if it was hieroglyphic, deciphering words letter by letter, doing consciously and laboriously what had been, before his stroke, unconscious and automatic. "I can make myself see that certain letter groupings are indeed familiar words, but that comes only after I have stared at the page."

Engel also started to bring in his other senses to complement the visual. He would move his tongue, almost unconsciously, as he read, tracing the shapes of letters on the roof of his mouth. This enables him to read a good deal faster (though it still might take him a month or more to read a book he might previously have read in an evening). Engel used other, more conventional help as well. His editor read the entire book to him once he had made his corrections to the first draft, and this was crucial in helping him to fix the overall structure of the book in his memory so that he could reorganize and work on it in his mind.

Some years ago I saw an eminent publisher, a very literate man, who had also, like Engel, developed visual alexia.

(Unlike Engel, he had developed it slowly, in consequence of a deteriorating brain disease, a gradual atrophy of the posterior visual parts of the brain—such a slow degeneration, a so-called focal atrophy, was also present in the alexia pianist whom I later saw.) This publisher found his whole orientation changing with this. He found himself becoming an auditory rather than a visual reader and writer; he devoured books on tape, and wrote by dictation—not only letters and memoranda but essays and an entire memoir. Engel, by contrast, has remained much more visual, and seems to prefer the tussle of trying to read books and write them visually, despite his difficulties with this.

The alexic pianist whom I wrote about ("The Case of Anna H."), after she became unable to read music, developed an extraordinary ability to listen to orchestral and choral works and arrange them for piano entirely in her mind, where before she would have needed manuscript paper and pencil to do this. The alexic publisher also told me that his power to "hear" what he had read or written, and to organize it in his mind, had steadily increased after his alexia. Such compensatory heightenings are almost universal in the blind—not only the congenitally blind but also those who have lost their sight later in life—and it seems likely that something similar occurs in the alexic, too.

Whatever the strategies employed—whether it is visually learning the shapes of letters anew, or copying and then "reading" them by means of tongue or finger movements, or developing heightened powers of auditory and conceptual memory, there seem to be many ways in which a person with alexia—especially a resourceful, verbal, highly motivated person like Engel—can get around the deficit, find new ways of doing things now that the old ways are unavailable. No doubt, too, there are changes in the brain underlying these adaptations, though these might be beyond the power of present brain imaging to show.

This is not to minimize the continuing impact of a condition like alexia in a world full of newspapers and books, maps and street signs, printed labels and directions on everything one uses—and above all, its impact on a writer like Engel, and the continuing, daily struggle to transcend it, one way or another. It is a struggle that calls for heroic determination and courage, as well as great resourcefulness, patience and, not least, humour—simply to survive, let alone to continue to write creatively, as Howard Engel has done. In *The Man Who Forgot How to Read*, Engel tells his story from the inside, with extraordinary insight, humour and intelligence. It is a story that is not only as fascinating as one of his own detective novels but a testament to the resilience and creative adaptation of one man and his brain.

Acknowledgements

ALTHOUGH THIS BOOK HAS MY NAME ON IT, it could not have been written without the help and encouragement of Grif Cunningham, Madeline Grant, Nancy Vichert, Don Summerhayes, Susan Milojevic and Bruce Johnson.

While I'm at it, I would also like to thank Bob Weaver, John Pearce, John Reeves, Cynthia Good, the Poets, and William, Charlotte and Jacob Engel.